"An urgent, biblically grounded su
tragedy of contemporary poverty i
personal stories to show both the v
and also how it is quite possible to
Factual. Practical. Engaging."
    —Ronald J. Sid

"I watched Everett en
hungry in my own com
systemic change, solid
below that challenges
one of America's most
the joy of walking alc
difference for the hungry of our neighborhood and nation."
            —Jimmy Dorrell, founder, Mission Waco/Mission World;
                pastor, Church Under the Bridge; president emeritus,
                Texas Christian Community Development Network

"We need this book! There are good books telling us why Christians should serve the poor, but they often leave one asking, 'How?' And there are good books that tell how a person or ministry has served the poor, but one wonders, 'Would that really work in my community?' In *I Was Hungry*, we learn how to actually serve the poor by seeing how serious Christians are doing just that in their own contexts."
                            —Todd L. Lake, Belmont University

"There is a considerable difference between being aware of our neighbors' needs and taking practical action to meet our neighbors' needs. Everett has devoted himself to bridging the gap through his leadership with the Texas Hunger Initiative, his own personal acts of service, and now through his words in *I Was Hungry*. For those wanting to participate in the daily service of praying 'on earth as it is in heaven,' *I Was Hungry* is a good place to begin."
                    —Andrew Greer, singer/songwriter and cohost
                        of the Amazon Prime show *Dinner Conversations*
                            with Mark Lowry and Andrew Greer

"Everett makes us see that 'other America' made up of needy people that is often invisible to those of us who live in our so-called affluent society. More important, he explains and demonstrates from his own experiences what we can do to minister to those who live there, whom Jesus called 'the least of these.' This book challenges us to act."
                            —Tony Campolo, Eastern University

"Confronted with America's hunger disaster—and its cultural, institutional, and spiritual causes—Everett asked, 'How can I help?' The Texas Hunger Initiative (THI) became his answer. *I Was Hungry* tells this remarkable story as well as the story of the gospel remarkably working its way through the world. Readers of this terrific book will find themselves asking, 'How can *I* help?'"

—**Jonathan Tran**, Baylor University

"In this book, which is full of practical wisdom and insight, Everett shares what it looks like not only to address hunger but also for Christians to partner together with their neighbors for the common good. Anyone who is interested in loving their neighbor, in feeding the hungry, and in being the church in and for the world should read this book. Everett is one of my heroes, and the stories and insights here capture much of why this is true."

—**Myles Werntz**, Hardin-Simmons University

"By the end of this book, readers will understand that they have a mentor and colleague in Jeremy who will help guide their own efforts to make their communities hunger free, as well as a friend who will help them guide their own personal spiritual journeys for a more just world."

—**Ambassador Tony P. Hall**

"*I Was Hungry* is a beautiful account of what our country needs more of: strong commitment to the common good, all through the lens of love. The pages are filled with enthralling stories that bring to life the realities of those struggling with food insecurity and poverty. It is God's voice that I hear throughout this poignant book. Hunger and poverty are problems we can make a serious dent in, and Jeremy helps us see how our mental models, perspective on God's rich abundance in our world, and a 'with, not for' plan of action can move us toward this goal as a nation."

—**Heather Reynolds**, Wilson Sheehan Lab for Economic Opportunities (LEO), University of Notre Dame

"Everett is one of the most talented people I have ever worked with and one of the finest people I know. He is also one of the country's leading experts on reducing food insecurity. This book is Everett at his best: drawing on his wealth of knowledge and experience, telling stories, and bringing people together to reduce hunger and poverty."

—**Victor J. Hinojosa**, Honors Program, Baylor University

"Everett does more than preach about the spiritual values our country so desperately needs—he lives them. On every single page, the honesty and authenticity with which he shares his journey yields inspiration for living a life that matters."

—**Billy Shore**, founder and executive chair of Share Our Strength

~~I WAS~~

~~HUNGRY~~

~~I WAS~~
~~HUNGRY~~

Cultivating Common Ground
to End an American Crisis

JEREMY K. EVERETT

FOREWORD BY DAVID BECKMANN

BrazosPress
a division of Baker Publishing Group
Grand Rapids, Michigan

© 2019 by Jeremy K. Everett

Published by Brazos Press
a division of Baker Publishing Group
PO Box 6287, Grand Rapids, MI 49516-6287
www.brazospress.com

Printed in the United States of America

Library of Congress Cataloging-in-Publication Data
Names: Everett, Jeremy K., 1975– author.
Title: I was hungry : cultivating common ground to end an American crisis / Jeremy K. Everett.
Description: Grand Rapids, MI : Brazos Press, a division of Baker Publishing Group, 2019. | Includes bibliographical references and index.
Identifiers: LCCN 2018054498 | ISBN 9781587434242 (pbk.)
Subjects: LCSH: Hunger—Religious aspects—Christianity. | Church and social problems—United States. | Church work with the poor—United States.
Classification: LCC BR115.H86 E94 2019 | DDC 261.8/3260973—dc23
LC record available at https://lccn.loc.gov/2018054498

ISBN 978-1-58743-443-3 (casebound)

Published in association with Creative Trust Literary Group, 210 Jamestown Park, Suite 200, Brentwood, TN 37027, www .creativetrust.com.

19 20 21 22 23 24 25   7 6 5 4 3 2 1

To Amy, Lucas, Sam, and Wyatt.
The loves of my life.

When the Son of Man comes in his glory, and all the angels with him, then he will sit on the throne of his glory. All the nations will be gathered before him, and he will separate people one from another as a shepherd separates the sheep from the goats, and he will put the sheep at his right hand and the goats at the left. Then the king will say to those at his right hand, "Come, you that are blessed by my Father, inherit the kingdom prepared for you from the foundation of the world; for I was hungry and you gave me food, I was thirsty and you gave me something to drink, I was a stranger and you welcomed me, I was naked and you gave me clothing, I was sick and you took care of me, I was in prison and you visited me." Then the righteous will answer him, "Lord, when was it that we saw you hungry and gave you food, or thirsty and gave you something to drink? And when was it that we saw you a stranger and welcomed you, or naked and gave you clothing? And when was it that we saw you sick or in prison and visited you?" And the king will answer them, "Truly I tell you, just as you did it to one of the least of these who are members of my family, you did it to me." Then he will say to those at his left hand, "You that are accursed, depart from me into the eternal fire prepared for the devil and his angels; for I was hungry and you gave me no food, I was thirsty and you gave me nothing to drink, I was a stranger and you did not welcome me, naked and you did not give me clothing, sick and in prison and you did not visit me." Then they also will answer, "Lord, when was it that we saw you hungry or thirsty or a stranger or naked or sick or in prison, and did not take care of you?" Then he will answer them, "Truly I tell you, just as you did not do it to one of the least of these, you did not do it to me." And these will go away into eternal punishment, but the righteous into eternal life.

Matthew 25:31–46

CONTENTS

Foreword by David Beckmann   xi

Acknowledgments   xiii

1. Disaster: *What I Learned from a Hurricane about Tackling the Hunger Disaster in America*   1

2. Broken Streetlights: *Finding Our Commonality amid Crisis*   16

3. A Priest and a Prostitute: *It Really Does Take Nearly Losing Your Life to Find It*   25

4. The People: *Finding Citizenship in the Right Kingdom*   40

5. The Desert: *Moving from Mind-Sets of Scarcity to Abundance*   53

6. Organize: *How a Shared Response Can Create Scalable Solutions to Our Communities' Greatest Social Challenges*   67

7. The West Side: *Once You Engage a Community, Fear Cannot Hold Out against Love*   85

8. Politics: *Searching for Consensus amid a Landscape of Contention*   103

Contents

9. Together at the Table: *The Texas Hunger Initiative's Story of Organizing a Systemic Response to Hunger*   118

10. Justice: *Our Cultural Moment to Find Common Ground for the Common Good*   136

   Notes   147

   Index   155

FOREWORD

Once I started the first chapter of this book, I had a hard time putting it down. Jeremy Everett is a great storyteller. And the overarching story of this book is God's call to Jeremy—to all of us actually—to end hunger.

I love the following story from Jeremy's student days. Late one night he watched an old movie about a young man named Francesco who felt called to give away all his possessions to people in need. Jeremy was captivated by Francesco's story even before he realized that the movie was about Francis of Assisi. Young Jeremy packed up all his possessions—even his beloved camping gear—and distributed them to homeless people in the city park.

Jeremy's radical gift didn't transform the lives of the people he encountered that day, but it was the start of Jeremy's pilgrimage from community organizing to his leadership in developing the Texas Hunger Initiative. This remarkable organization helps communities, government programs, and companies work together to reduce the scourge of hunger all across the great state of Texas. Their collaborative efforts have provided countless meals for Texans who struggle with hunger. This book explains how caring people in any state or community can have the same impact.

Jeremy also introduces us to some of the individuals who cope with hunger. He and his family lived next door to Lupe. She and her husband struggled to provide for their children, and her premature death due to lack of adequate health care only intensified their predicament. Jeremy tells us about a student who let his grades slip so he would have access to food during summer school. Jeremy explains how elderly men and women in El Paso, who have worked hard at low-paying jobs all their lives, can't afford groceries now that they aren't able to work any longer.

Jeremy is now a leader in a spiritual and political movement to end hunger. He knows from experience that unlikely allies can come together to solve this problem. He believes this can and should happen nationwide. We can end hunger and, at the same time, help to heal the crippling divisions that now threaten the security and well-being of all of us.

David Beckmann
President, Bread for the World
and the Alliance to End Hunger

ACKNOWLEDGMENTS

Amy Miley Everett, you matter to me. I am grateful beyond words that you are in my life and that I am in yours. You have traveled with me to places I did not know existed, whether that was the depths of our human nature or forgotten communities inside and outside the US. I am grateful for your companionship, heart, and insight. I am fortunate to have you as my fellow sojourner in life. Lucas, Sam, and Wyatt, you have taught me more about love and how to love than I ever knew was possible. I am so grateful to be your father and to have a front row seat in your amazing lives.

Mom and Dad, thank you for a lifetime's worth of encouragement, discipline, and love. Your faithful witness and commitment to the cause of Christ are inspiring. Your lessons on leadership have had a profound impact on my life, and—most of all—thanks for not killing me during my teenage years. Rachel, you are a sibling I wish everyone could have. You are intelligent, passionate, and willing to drop everything to help your brother in times of need. Thanks for your faithful witness at a young age that challenged my preconceived notions of life and pointed me toward justice.

The Miley crew, I hit the jackpot with a family to marry into. You have taken me in as one of your own, taught me to deepen my faith and embrace my love of the outdoors, and introduced me to fly-fishing. Your passionate love for each other is enviable.

The Texas Hunger Initiative team, both past and present, I still cannot believe you have agreed to join the cause with me. You are an incredibly sharp, committed, and focused group of people who have given yourselves over to the cause of ending hunger and poverty. Thank you for all you have taught me about leadership for social change and all your inspiration for this book. Thank you to our administrative team for allowing me the freedom to take time to write about our experience and holding down the fort in my absence.

Kasey Ashenfelter and Erin Nolen, I especially want to thank you both for your many edits, for shaping the ideas on the pages of this book, and for the countless hours of research you did to ensure the content was accurate. This book would not have been written without your help.

Kathy Helmers, my agent at Creative Trust, thank you for all of the time you put into this book to make sure I was articulating on paper what I was saying to you over the phone during our many phone calls. Your time, energy, and edits helped improve this book. Additionally, I would like to thank Elizabeth Cauthorn and Sheryl Fullerton for your guidance, encouragement, and connection during the publishing process.

Brazos Press/Baker Academic at Baker Publishing Group have been a great team from the early stages of this book's inception. In particular, I am appreciative of the guidance of Dave Nelson, whose committed energy and wisdom—along with a chorus of others—helped bring forth this book from my mind onto the following pages.

My thanks to all of the following: Suzii Paynter, Jon Singletary, and Diana Garland for taking a chance on me and this crazy project; Don Arispe, Bill Ludwig, and the many mentors I have had along the way for offering wisdom and a safe place to think through new ways of seeking justice; the West Side community of San Antonio for your acceptance of a lanky white dude wanting to make a difference; my friends from Gandalf's Lair, Sean, Cam, Erin, Britt, Wes; and the rest of our Truett crew—our formation during that season of life still fuels me to this day.

I realize that nothing I have done or written has been done alone. I am continually inspired by people I meet every day. I am grateful for the many people who have poured so much into my life without asking for anything in return. I am grateful to God that he still walks alongside of me and has not given up on me despite my selfishness, thickheadedness, and sense of entitlement. I am grateful.

DISASTER

What I Learned from a Hurricane about
Tackling the Hunger Disaster in America

Katrina

In the days and hours following the landfall of Hurricane Katrina in August 2005, while everybody was holding their breath hoping the levees would hold, waterways were already completely full, New Orleans was flooding, people were being displaced, and the death toll was beginning its gruesome climb.

As I watched the story unfold on television, I remembered hearing in the 1990s from an executive at the Federal Emergency Management Agency (FEMA), a close friend of my father's, about two possible emergencies for which the nation was drastically unprepared: a tsunami hitting California and wiping out urban centers along the coast and a category four or five hurricane hitting New Orleans. Because the city lay below sea level, its decades-old levees would be no match for such a powerful

1

storm. Once the levees broke, he predicted the resulting floods would be devastating.

We all saw the horrific pictures captured by news crews when the levees finally gave way: people scrambling to their roof-tops hoping to be rescued; thousands clamoring to get into the Superdome, which was already in bad shape with its roof blown off; store owners armed with guns trying to ward off looters, people desperate to grab anything within reach.

One scene that remains particularly vivid in my memory is of people stranded on a bridge, where they had climbed because it was the only structure not under water. Because of the magnitude of the disaster, emergency responders were unable to reach them for five days. Helicopters dropped water and a little bit of food to help them maintain some level of survival.

Once some roads were able to be cleared, school buses, he-licopters, planes, ambulances, and charter buses descended on the city to transport New Orleans residents to other cities, and the chaos continued. Because each vehicle had a limited number of seats, some families could not all board the same one, and since this happened before cell phones and social media were prolific, when people were split up, they had no idea where their family members and friends were being sent. When a bus left New Orleans, no one knew where it was going; it just left town. Evacuation vehicles were routed to Dallas, Fort Worth, Okla-homa City, Houston, San Antonio—any city that had room. Oftentimes bus drivers would be heading in one direction only to find out that they needed to change course because their destination city was full. So a mom and daughter could end up in San Antonio while the family's father and brother were in Oklahoma City, and neither side had the ability to figure out where the other was. There was no tracking system for individuals once they got onto a bus or as they checked into a shelter. People simply arrived hoping their loved ones were safe and they would be reunited soon.

As people were evacuated from New Orleans to other cities, massive shelters, such as the Houston Astrodome, became full.

Organizers quickly began to realize that not everyone could live in a general population shelter with thousands of other people. Infants and people who were mentally or physically disabled needed a more direct level of care than could be afforded them in a general population shelter. They needed to be moved out.

The organization where I worked, a Baptist social service agency, was called on. FEMA asked us to drop what we were doing and open up medical special needs shelters. These were smaller shelters for a particular part of the population that needed more intense care.

I was sent to manage a small shelter on the south side of San Antonio in a church gymnasium. It was an extremely old facility, and I had often joked that it was probably the first church gymnasium in Texas. The air-conditioning was shoddy, the kitchen was mediocre, and the bathroom facilities weren't great. We had room for about 150 people.

Before we were completely ready, buses full of people began to arrive, and the chaos from the storm continued. Because we were a special needs shelter, most of the people coming to us had no real ability to take care of themselves because of their physical limitations. They were hungry, and the many who were diabetic hadn't had their insulin. Their sugar levels had been thrown off balance to the point that many of them were hardly able to put together a coherent sentence. Most of them had soiled themselves en route because the buses didn't have bathrooms or they were physically unable to use them without assistance. By the time they arrived, they were hot and sweaty after waiting for days to be evacuated. The smell was horrible; it was the smell of people who had soiled themselves, been exposed to heat and humidity for days, and then cooped up on public transit for hours. Those who were still coherent were mortified. They had a blank stare in their eyes like that of a soldier returning from the horrors of battle.

Some of the arrivals had been among those stranded on the bridge, including a seventy-five-year-old woman who had broken her hip during the evacuation from her home. She should have gone to a hospital, but by that point all the hospitals in San Antonio were full—both the hospital rooms and the hallways were overflowing with people. Our shelter was a sea of army cots, but we had one lone hospital bed that we were able to give to her. Because of her hip, she couldn't walk, so whenever she needed to use the restroom, three evacuees and I would each take a corner of her bedsheet, lift her up, and carry her to the bathroom. I can only imagine how painful that was for her. It was almost a week before we could get her seen by a doctor.

Another man who was wheelchair-bound felt humiliated each time he had to use the restroom because we had to physically take him to the facilities and help him with all the intimate details involved with relieving oneself. We did not know him, and he did not know us, and the shame and humiliation he was experiencing were evident in his facial expressions.

The work was exhausting—eighteen-hour days, six or seven days a week, for months until we could get people back home or find a more permanent place for them to stay. The emotional toll was more severe. I had been working and living among impoverished conditions for years, but I had never seen tragedy on this level in my life. Obviously, our peril as first responders paled in comparison to that of the evacuees.

Our agency was responsible for connecting volunteers with tasks that were actually helpful. People really wanted to help out. They donated clothes and all sorts of goods, but what we really needed was a coordinated food schedule. People were arriving at all times of day, and finding enough volunteers and resources just to provide meals for people was a challenge. The health department came in and said that the people staying at the shelter couldn't go in the kitchen; only volunteers could enter. Since volunteers were needed all over the city, trying to find enough hands to provide food was a major challenge.

Additionally, doctors were not available because of the scale of the need, so our small team without medical experience had to learn how to administer medication. A whole host of the population needed diabetes medication, and figuring out how to get it for them was difficult.

Everything about the hurricane, including our response to it, was chaotic. The first responders—fire departments, police departments, and emergency medical technicians—all spoke different work languages and struggled to coordinate their efforts. No one knew who was in charge or how to give directions. Evacuations were directionless, shelters were overcrowded, medication was inadequate, and volunteers were disorganized. Everything was a mess, and what we desperately needed was a coordinated response.

The Power of a Shared Response

When another devastating hurricane season hit three years after Katrina, I had a chance to see from the inside out what a difference proactive coordination can make.

By the time Hurricanes Gustav and Ike blew into Louisiana and Texas, the federal government, through FEMA and Homeland Security, already knew it would need to do a better job of coordinating across sectors. The agencies implemented a new training process to do this. A manual was written up for medical special needs shelters so that people knew how to manage them not only in San Antonio but also across the country. Many of my coworkers were able to use their expertise, developed during Hurricane Katrina, to contribute to the manual. Though we all were trained, we all also had to speak the same language. In typical government fashion, the federal agencies developed a new language for us to learn, mainly composed of acronyms. We began to understand everyone's unique role, who was responsible for what, and how to orchestrate a coordinated response. For example, we learned that an incident commander was in charge. It didn't matter who that incident commander was, what his or her title was when that person wasn't the incident commander, or who showed up; even if the president of the United States arrived, the incident commander was still in charge. We were all given roles to execute precisely.

During Hurricanes Gustav and Ike, I managed several shelters in east Texas and a Veterans Affairs Hospital shelter on Kelly Air Force Base in San Antonio. When people arrived at the shelter, we could code them and identify where their loved ones were if they had been split up during the evacuation. We also had a plan to reconnect them with their families. The federal government developed contracts with helicopter, airplane, and bus companies. They rerouted interstates prior to the hurricanes so that both the eastbound and westbound lanes could be utilized to get people out of the disaster-prone area as quickly as possible. Shelters were no longer rough-and-tumble. Now we had not only a generator but also a backup generator in case the power failed. In one of the shelters I managed, we even had a makeshift intensive care unit where we literally had the ability to put people on life support. Teams of physicians and nurses worked around the clock in our shelters. I, with a degree in theology, was no longer responsible for giving insulin to diabetics. We had a full pharmacy in each shelter so we could give people medications as they needed them. We were able to offer meals four times a day so that even those who arrived in the middle of the night could receive some food. We had contracts with restaurants and food service companies to provide meals to ensure that everyone was taken care of. We no longer had to worry about whether or not we were going to have food for people the next day. We even had laundry services set up so people could clean their soiled clothes. It was a completely different experience.

Ultimately, what was important was that there was a grand plan to get people back home. We knew that people could not go back to their communities until grocery stores opened or else they wouldn't have food. We knew that communities needed to be cleaned up and that people needed to have access to their homes to see what had survived the storm.

The work was still exhausting and still required all hands on deck, but it was a coordinated response that made the difference.

Stranded by the Hunger Disaster

For the past twenty years, I have traveled the country and other parts of the world observing, researching, and addressing hunger and poverty. Much of what I have learned about addressing hunger and poverty is similar to what I learned by working in disaster response. The problem is often overwhelming, and we need to find a way to work together in a coordinated response to address these issues that have been around for thousands of years. Years after Hurricanes Katrina, Gustav, and Ike, while living and working in San Antonio, I was offered the opportunity to put these ideas to the test when I was asked by Texas Baptists to start an organization focused specifically on co-ordinating a collective response to hunger, the Texas Hunger Initiative (THI).

The premise was that hunger and poverty are too large and too complex to address alone. We would all need to work together in a coordinated capacity if we wanted to make a dent in them, much less end them. We also knew that we had a cultural problem. Our nation tends toward blaming the hungry and poor for their plight rather than walking alongside them to find solutions. Blaming the poor for their poverty only adds insult to injury and is largely an inaccurate diagnosis. We also had a spiritual problem. Jesus spoke frequently about loving our neighbor in practical and tangible ways, such as providing food for the hungry, but hunger in Texas was more prevalent than in almost any other state in the nation or in any developed country around the world. We needed a stronger understanding of our collective call to love God and our neighbor, and we needed to move with a sense of urgency, as I would soon learn.

As I was transitioning into this new position, I was told I needed to meet Pastor Dan Trevino, because his congregation was providing food for the hungry. Dan's congregation was on the South Side of San Antonio, a sister neighborhood to the West Side, where I was living. Dan spoke to me about his congregation's ministries in the community. They had a charter school that used the church's education building, a food pantry, a community garden, and literacy and employment classes. If you can think of an idea for ministry, Dan and his church were probably doing it.

As we talked and toured the church, Dan told me about a formative experience. He said that he and his sons had come to the church one Saturday morning before dawn to make breakfast tacos for the elders in the congregation. When they pulled into the church parking lot, the headlights of his van revealed children in the church's dumpster. He and his sons were startled, and so were the children in the dumpster. The kids tried to get out of the dumpster and run away, but Dan was able to get to them and calm their fears. He invited them into the church's kitchen and made them breakfast tacos before the elders arrived. Once they were full, he began to ask them why they were in the dumpster. Slowly, the boys began to open up and told him that they did not have any food in the house, so they had snuck out while it was still dark to rummage through the dumpster to see if they could find something to eat.

I was stunned. Dan's church wasn't far from the Riverwalk and all that we enjoy visiting in San Antonio. Yet there were children in his community so impoverished that they were rummaging through a dumpster to find food. This was a story I expected to hear about the developing world, but downtown San Antonio? My shock led to dismay. How could our nation passively let children experience such extreme circumstances? How could the church?

Gandhi called poverty the harshest form of violence. I believe hunger is the harshest form of poverty. Hunger is debilitating. It stimulates physical pain, anger, lethargy, and depression. It will keep you up at night and ironically cause drowsiness during the day. I can only imagine the shame and humiliation parents experience when their children miss meals. One of our primary responsibilities is to provide a stable household for our families. We want to make sure they have food, a consistent place to sleep, and a loving environment. If we were unable to provide them with three meals a day and a place to sleep, we would probably feel inadequate and ashamed.

These dumpster-diving kids were no different than the hurricane survivors on the bridge: they had been stranded by tragedy. Travel to any urban or rural impoverished community and you will find similar stories everywhere. Today in the United States, over forty million Americans are food insecure (or at risk of hunger). According to the US Department of Agriculture (USDA), this means that at times during the year, these individuals live in households that are uncertain of having or are unable to acquire enough food to meet the needs of all their family members because they have insufficient money or other resources for food.[1] Nearly one out of six children in the US live in a food-insecure household. That number is one out of two in south Texas.[2] Furthermore, economic inequality is the worst it has been in modern American history. A person working a full-time job and getting paid minimum wage earns less than the federal poverty line, and the poverty line is an inaccurate underrepresentation of true poverty.

I Was Hungry

Most Christians are probably familiar with Jesus's teaching in Matthew 25: "For I was hungry and you gave me food, I was thirsty and you gave me something to drink, I was a stranger and you welcomed me, I was naked and you gave me clothing, I was sick and you took care of me, I was in prison and you visited me" (vv. 35–36).

This is the only apocalyptic (or end-of-the-world) scene in Matthew.[3] Jesus the King has returned, and he is sitting on the throne. This is the final judgment. All people are gathered, and

Jesus is separating them—the sheep and the goats, the righteous from the accused. To the astonishment of the people gathered, "the criterion for judgment is not confession of faith in Christ. Nothing is said of grace, justification, or the forgiveness of sins." Instead, what matters is whether a person has acted with love and cared for the needy. These acts are not just extra credit but "constitute the decisive criterion for judgment."[4] Essentially, "when the people respond or fail to respond to human need, they are in fact responding, or failing to respond, to Christ."[5]

The calling of the faithful is clear: feed the hungry and you will live.

But we don't rush to rescue these sufferers the way we did when Katrina wreaked its havoc. A hurricane we can understand. Poverty? Hunger? Many of us believe people just need to get a job and quit complaining. Unfortunately, this type of narrow thinking has only worsened our current situation. The truth is that the realities of hunger and poverty are complex. People experience hunger in our nation typically because they live in poverty. They are therefore forced to decide between purchasing food or medicine, paying for housing or making a car payment, and so on.

West Texas

As we saw with the emergency responders and volunteers for Hurricane Katrina, a lack of effective communication between organizations makes it impossible to efficiently organize a response to disaster. Poverty is a disaster, and those responding to it are often speaking different languages and on different wavelengths. The faith-based sector doesn't know what the public sector is doing; the public sector doesn't know what the corporate sector is involved with; and many philanthropists don't know what the federal poverty programs are funding.

This disaster is magnified when we have an unorganized response. Although there are numerous federal nutrition and antipoverty programs, oftentimes these agencies lack strong communication and program integration with agencies working with the same populations on state or local levels. Not to mention that churches and nonprofits often do their own thing. Furthermore, nonprofits, who should be strategically aligned and working together seamlessly, often compete against one another because they are applying to the same potential funders, who have a limited amount of funding.

This does not mean there is a lack of compassionate people working tirelessly to address hunger and poverty. Quite the opposite. Amazing people and amazing organizations are doing great things, even if addressing hunger and poverty is not a national priority. Unfortunately, due to the high needs of communities across the country, these compassionate responders simply do not have the bandwidth to identify key organizations to partner with in ways they collectively desire. The result is an uncoordinated response, creating a massive gap in services across the nation despite the numerous efforts to fill this gap.

To try to combat this chaos, in the first year of the Texas Hunger Initiative, as part of our effort to build collaboration, my friends at the USDA, the food banks, Texas state agencies, and Texas congregations decided to identify pilot communities across the state where we could organize a collaborative response to address food insecurity. Our attempt would be modeled after what we had learned by addressing disasters together. Initially, we identified over four thousand organizations in Texas doing something about hunger, yet we still had five and a half million food-insecure people. Many of the organizations we visited told us of their desire to partner with other groups, but the need they were addressing every day was so great they simply did not have the time to step back to find ways to work with other organizations. This resulted in duplicated efforts and gaps of services that no one was aware of.

Our group traveled around Texas to hold town hall meetings to announce our vision for a hunger-free state and begin galvanizing communities across sectors by asking the non-profits, churches, businesses, school districts, and local governments to work together to address hunger in their communities. These meetings were successful, and we were quickly able to identify several pilot communities in which to try out our collaborative model.

Then, about midway into that year, I received a phone call from Mary and Carol, two women from Southland Baptist Church in San Angelo, Texas. I knew of the church because my father-in-law had pastored there twenty-five years earlier, and I had met Mary and Carol when my wife and I had visited San Angelo.

On the phone that morning, they spoke with a sense of earnestness and urgency.

"Jeremy, three of San Angelo's large manufacturing plants just closed. So many people lost their jobs, and we know many San Angelo children are going hungry because of it, especially when school is out."

"Mary, I am sorry to hear that. How can I help?"

"We heard about THI and wanted to become one of your pilot communities."

"Well, unfortunately, we have already chosen our pilot communities."

"Well, can you add one more?" At the time, there were only a couple of us working at THI, and we did not have the ability to take on an additional community.

"We really can't right now. We just don't have enough staff. Check back with us next year. Hopefully, we will have more staff members by then so we can assist you."

My answer did not work for them. Instead of hanging up the phone, they repeated their story as if I simply hadn't heard it the first time. This time they spoke a little louder, with more urgency and even sprinkled with a bit of hostility. "Jeremy, three of our plants closed. People are out of work, which means their kids aren't eating!" As if I did not fully understand what they communicated the first time.

They were clearly persistent, and I could see that I was not going to get off the phone unless I obliged—or came up with something for them to do. So I asked them to complete a community assessment. The assessment typically takes quite a while, at least several months. My assumption was that Mary and Carol either would be overwhelmed with the amount of work and simply go on their way or that they would take the next year to complete the assessment and call me back then.

"Thank you, Jeremy," Mary said.

Carol chimed in, "We will call you back soon!"

Three weeks later, they called me back! Mary informed me that they had completed the assessment and asked plainly, "So can we be a pilot community now?"

I laughed with sheer amazement and said, "I think you already are."

Mary and Carol disclosed that, although there were ten thousand children on the free and reduced-price lunch program in their county, the community provided only one thousand meals throughout the entire summer of 2009. They knew that children were going hungry in the summer, and they were ready to do something about it. Needless to say, we arranged for our group to go to San Angelo.

When we arrived, we were met by a group that included the school district superintendent and school board members, city council officials and the mayor, church leaders, nonprofit directors, people from the business community, a representative from a congressman's office, and concerned citizens. These people from different political parties and religious affiliations were ready to get to work for the children of Tom Green County. After our town hall meeting, people met weekly over the next several months to plan for the upcoming summer. They knew that they each had something they could offer and developed a strategy. One group would cook the meals, another would deliver them to a site. Then another group would be a host site, while yet another would provide activities to encourage children and families to come. In the summer of 2010, Tom Green County served nearly twenty thousand meals to children.

Mary and Carol are somewhat unusual in their tenacity. These two women have spent much of their lives in San Angelo, cultivating trust by advocating for those on the margins. So when they called community leaders to tell them of the food insecurity epidemic among their children, the leaders were willing to listen and respond with the same sense of urgency I had heard over the phone during that initial call. West Texans have a saying about reliability: You can hang your hat on that! Mary and Carol are as reliable as they come.

Mary and Carol were also wise enough to know that one church, one school, one business, or one nonprofit could not meet the needs of so many food-insecure children. They knew that strength would come only if the community worked together. They learned sustainable social change happens by cultivating trust, collaborating across denominational and political lines, and committing to the cause of the poor and hungry. They proved that working together was both possible and pragmatic. They also put flesh on Jesus's command to care for the poor.

Triumph or Tragedy?

Our team at THI works at the federal, state, and local levels to bridge the gap between the resources that exist and the people who need them most. We didn't invent the model. In fact, shortly after those early town hall meetings, a new theory of social change called collective impact was popularized in the *Stanford Social Innovation Review*.[6] Collective impact—which espouses a "commitment of a group of important actors from different sectors to a common agenda for solving a specific social problem" using a structured form of collaboration[7]—coupled with our experiences addressing poverty and responding to disasters, gave us a framework to increase access to existing programs, maximize the efforts of charities and volunteers,

build collaboration to ensure community members are working together, and strengthen all of this work with university
research. What we have been brewing in our Texas laboratory
can be replicated and indeed is being replicated in other states
and communities throughout our nation.

In this book, I will weave together stories of triumph and
tragedy with research and practical solutions for addressing
hunger and poverty in our communities. I hope you will walk
away with a greater understanding of the plight of people in
America who struggle with food insecurity and that your greater
understanding will elicit a compassionate response. I also want
you to be equipped with resources and solutions to address the
hunger and poverty crisis in your community. Throughout the
book I will illustrate these ideas with stories from my journey
and how I came to some of the conclusions I draw in the book.
We are a nation on a dangerous path. My hope is that by working together to build trust and collaborating to address hunger in
our communities we will recognize our common humanity and
put aside the hateful rhetoric that is pervasive in our nation.

How might the Spirit of God move if we came out of our
silos and chose collaboration for the common good over contention in order to rescue our stranded neighbors abandoned by
the storms of hunger and poverty? In a time when some of us
have way too much food and others way too little, it is a tragedy
to argue over policies and politics and even Bible verses while
people on the bridge are waiting for an airlift.

So let's turn social awareness into social activation, build
hunger-free communities, and end the systemic hunger disaster
in America. I know we can do it, because I have been privileged to see progress happen both top down and ground up: a
coalition of the willing, crossing ideological divides instead of
widening them, coming together at the table of collaboration
for the hungry. Triumph or tragedy? The choice is ours.

2

BROKEN STREETLIGHTS

Finding Our Commonality amid Crisis

In 2004, my family and I moved to the West Side of San Antonio. In San Antonio, the West Side was not considered the "good" neighborhood. The median income on the West Side was about $19,000 per household, and the average house had three generations living in it. Only 3 percent of the community had access to a personal computer, and the highest performing high school had a 50 percent dropout rate. Despite—or maybe because of—the neighborhood's troubles, I was about to start working there, and we decided to buy a house in the community.

Not long after moving in, we became friends with our neighbors Lupe and Luis.[1] They were devout Catholics and had a large family. Lupe and Luis, their eight children, and Lupe's two elderly parents all shared the same home. Four of their kids were about the same age as our children, and they would come to our home to play with our two young sons when they would get out of school. Sometimes the kids were dirty, hungry, and playing without shoes. (We suspected that their water would regularly get turned off, that there was not sufficient food in their house, particularly toward the end of the month, and that shoes were saved for special occasions.) They would come over and play games inside and run around outside. Their favorite thing to do was to play with our water hose, especially during the hot summer months in south Texas. They also loved it when my wife would bring out fresh fruit to eat or when we had extra change and let them buy something from the ice-cream truck, because when school was out for the summer, those snacks were possibly the only thing they got to eat during the day.

In addition to raising her children, Lupe was the primary caregiver to her wheelchair-bound parents. Every morning Lupe would get her kids ready for school and then help her parents onto the bus so they could go to a neighborhood senior center, where they would spend part of their day. After her parents were gone for the day, Lupe would volunteer at her kids' schools. She knew that the only way her children could escape the harsh realities of poverty was through education, and her goal was for each of them to graduate high school and then, hopefully, attend San Antonio Community College. This wasn't her goal for just her own children. Lupe wanted to see all the children in the community succeed, so she diligently championed education as a committed volunteer.

Luis worked a full-time job and had an additional job on the weekends, a common practice among community members. Most people in the neighborhood did not have full-time employment with one employer, so they would piece together two or three jobs, sometimes working sixty to eighty hours a week, when they were lucky.

One day, after we had been neighbors for a few years, Lupe got an ear infection, but she did not have health insurance or a doctor. Her family had only one small car that Luis used to get to work each day. So, of course, Lupe's ear infection went untreated. Eventually it became unbearably painful, so after getting her kids ready and sending her parents off, Lupe got on a bus herself and went to a downtown hospital, where she sat in the lobby of the emergency room all day waiting to be seen. She still had not been seen when it was time for her to catch a bus so she could make it back home in time to greet her kids after school, so she left, still untreated.

Later that evening, Lupe's eardrum ruptured. The infection went into her brain and caused her to go into a coma. Lupe never woke up.

The evening after she died, Luis and his sons made the rounds in our neighborhood collecting money for Lupe's burial. We stood together on my front porch, and as he cried with his head buried in his hands, Luis kept repeating, "What am I going to do? What am I going to do?"

Poverty in the US is incredibly complicated, involving myriad underlying issues such as wage rates, health care access, housing costs, and hunger. We often talk about people without health insurance or people living with hunger or families in poverty as if there are subgroups dealing with each isolated issue. The reality is that the same families live with all of these conditions. Lupe and Luis and their family were food insecure, were underemployed, lacked health insurance, and so on. When I think of Lupe's story and the widespread poverty in our country, I am reminded of Franklin Delano Roosevelt's famous quotation: "The test of our progress is not whether we add more to the abundance of those who have much; it is whether we provide enough for those who have too little."[2] Similarly, the prophet Isaiah warned us "to share your bread with the hungry, and bring the homeless poor into your house; when you see the naked, to cover them, and not to hide yourself from your own kin" (Isa. 58:7). Instead of heeding the wisdom of these statements, we have built economic and justice systems that are geared toward those who have and control the most, not toward families like Lupe's. In 2017, I read that President Trump's first seventeen cabinet member picks are financially worth more than forty-six million American households—not people but households.[3] Unfortunately, some streams of the church have found ways of endorsing this disparity, despite the warnings of Scripture and the teachings of Jesus.

Springhill Paper

The 2016 presidential election, the rise of populism,[4] and the spotlight being put on the plight of southern, rural poverty, predominantly among white households, caused me to reflect on the small town that was home to my grandparents in the latter part of their lives: Springhill, Louisiana. Springhill is emblematic of the continuously bad economic decisions we the people (not just our elected leaders) have been making during the past half century, often in the name of progress. To be fair to Springhill, it was not the only community to follow this path. Many communities have followed the path I am about to describe.

Springhill is best known for Springhill Paper. The community, like many small southern towns, used to be home to small farmers whose sustenance came from cotton, with vegetable and small animal production predominantly reserved for the family. Once Springhill Paper opened, the cash crop evolved to pine trees, which were harvested for the paper mill. Slowly, land was bought up by larger investors and completely converted to the production of pine trees for the paper mill. Naturally, as people left their family farms, they migrated to the paper mill for employment.

As a child I would get excited to see a box of Springhill paper on my teacher's desk, because I knew my grandparents lived there. And when we traveled to visit my grandparents, we knew we were getting close when the smell of the plant overtook the car and we saw the plumes of smoke billowing into the sky above the lines of pine trees.

When we visited, the town seemed to be thriving. My grandfather's church was always full, and buildings were kept in good repair. But beginning in the 1990s, Springhill Paper, by then bought out by a larger multinational corporation, began closing down parts of the plant. Slowly but surely the layoffs began to take a toll on the community. Today the plant is almost completely closed, and the town is only a shadow of what it was during my childhood. The families who were once proud farming families, then proud manufacturing families, are now out of work. The fortunate few are able to commute to Shreveport, an hour away, to work in the casinos.

Many residents of Springhill likely need government support to survive, but do not be mistaken, it is not because they do not want to work or because government programs are so enticing that people would rather depend on them than be gainfully employed. Anyone suggesting that a social safety net existence is something that people prefer has never spent quality time with the poor. Though it is true that a collective depression robs people of their hope and ambition to improve their situation, as they look around, there seem to be no good options.

For many families like Lupe's and communities like Springhill, the deck appears to be stacked against them. Their schools have high dropout rates, and families lack sufficient food and health insurance. Opportunities for upward mobility are scarce, if not altogether nonexistent. The American myth of pulling yourself up by your bootstraps evidently does not apply to people who cannot afford boots.

The great irony in the rise of the populist movement in the United States is that our impoverished white brothers and sisters are often pitted against our impoverished brothers and sisters of color. Yet both want the same thing. They want to be able to feed their families. They want economic opportunity so they can create better lives for themselves and their families. Unfortunately, when we are in desperate times it is easy to point a finger at those who are other and fail to address the true problems.

This is not a new problem. These families have been pitted against one another since Reconstruction after the Civil

War. Many poor Southern whites were forced out of jobs and relocated when slavery was abolished and Union soldiers occupied the South. Southerners love to talk about heritage and reflect on these stories as if they happened a decade ago. This is not an indictment on anyone but a factor in the equation of our nation's current contempt. We have to find a way toward healing and economic wholeness for all people in our country. After all, residents of Springhill and the West Side have more in common than they care to admit.

Our First Step

In this time of contention, why should we address hunger instead of other pressing issues facing our nation? It does seem that racial hatred, the threat of nuclear war, and climate change are more pressing issues. Perhaps they are—though I do believe poverty will be one of the central issues our generation will be judged by in the decades to come. I will explain more about that later. For now, here is something I learned in my early days doing community development, why I think hunger is a solvable problem, and why I think the time to do so is now.

In those early years, I came across the broken streetlight theory. The theory is based on a scenario in which a community developer has just started working in a neighborhood and must garner the trust of the community. Knowing that one way to do so is to identify a winnable issue around which to organize the community, the developer knocks on doors in the community to ask people what they see as strengths in the neighborhood and also what they see as ailing it. People respond with worry about their health care bills, the erosion of livable wage employment, and that the school's system of standardized testing is putting their children at a disadvantage.

These issues are important to the community and the community developer, but they are simply too big to take on first, especially when the developer lacks established trust and has yet to build a powerful network of individuals and organizations. But, the theory continues, in addition to the large-scale issues, the developer is also repeatedly told that the streetlight on the corner has been broken for some time, and a drug dealer sells drugs under it. As a result, parents do not feel it is safe for their children to play in the front yard anymore. *This* is a winnable issue. The developer recruits the community to go to the electric company to request that the streetlight be fixed. The electric company obliges. The streetlight is fixed, the drug dealer moves on, and it is safe for children to play in front yards again. Not only does the community get a win and a feeling of safety but the organizer gains a significant amount of trust. Once trust is established and the community feels empowered, they are able to take on more difficult issues—together.

Poverty is incredibly complex. And people in our nation are literally willing to kill one another to strengthen their ideological agendas, but hunger has consistently been a uniting issue for our nation and around the globe. Perhaps this is because of the leftover food we throw away daily, the images we see of starving children around the world, or the simplicity of serving a brother or sister a meal in comparison to helping them navigate the health-care system or finding them a home. Whatever the reason may be, hunger is the broken streetlight of poverty issues, and organizing a systemic response to address hunger is an important step toward the larger goal of economic opportunity for all people. Mary, Carol, and the San Angelo community demonstrated that when we address hunger collaboratively, doing so can bring together people from all walks of life—Republicans and Democrats, Catholics and Baptists, Muslims and the Jews, teachers and CEOs—and can create community across ideological divides while addressing an issue of paramount importance.

That does not mean that it will be easy or that we stop there. Ending hunger is an important first step toward these larger goals of ending systemic poverty and becoming better stewards of creation. Like the community organizer and the neighborhood in the broken streetlight theory, we can learn to trust one another again by working to reduce hunger, which will then empower us to face these other debilitating problems with confidence that we can overcome what ails us.

Common Ground

If it is true that we are all created in the image of God, then we likely have more in common with one another than we realize. When we identify this commonality, it becomes much easier to join in collaborative efforts to strengthen impoverished households that not only improve lives but also build trust. And when we care about people and issues of injustice more than about being right, we all can win. In so doing, we create change that is sustainable because it is built on the premise of love of neighbor and involves everyone's input.

Unfortunately, at a time of unrest in our nation and around the world, a time when we need our leaders to come together for the common good, our society is more fragmented than it has been at any time since the civil rights era, if not the Civil War, which practically ensures that the systemic problems of domestic hunger and poverty will persist. To be clear, while we spend our time politically bickering, our children and our elderly are quietly going without food.

Although our nation continues toward a contentious divide, we as people of faith can take solace that, as Martin Luther King Jr. prophetically witnessed, "The arc of a moral universe bends towards justice."[5]

If Scripture is correct, we as a nation and a world will be judged based on how we treat the hungry and poor, not on whether we improved the quality of life of those of us who have much. Scripture and history repeat this claim over and over, and we must listen, not to the populist uprising but to what is underneath it, the desperation in the voices here and all over the world that are shouting for help, whether they be the voices of Syrian refugees, children escaping violence in El Salvador, or the poor in Detroit, San Angelo, or the West Side of San Antonio. This is the kingdom of God that Christ calls us to. This is our task as people of faith.

Most of us want children to have ample access to food and adults to be able to find work that can sustain a family. I also imagine most of us believe that the processes toward these ends do not have to pit us against one another. There seems to be a collective intuition that working together to solve our country's and our world's greatest woes is a better path forward than the mean-spiritedness and vitriol we see in our politicians, preachers, political commentators, and endless amounts of social media posts. Let's work together across our ideological divides to address hunger, cultivating trust that will put our nation on a path toward economic opportunity for all people.

A PRIEST AND A PROSTITUTE

It Really Does Take Nearly
Losing Your Life to Find It

I grew up as the son of a preacher man. My father followed his father's footsteps into pastoral ministry in the Baptist church. He joked that he had only three years' worth of sermons, so every three to four years we moved so my dad could pastor a new congregation.

Each time we moved I experienced life on the margins. Sometimes it may not have lasted very long, but inevitably I would begin a year at school with the painful feeling of wondering who I would sit with in the cafeteria during lunchtime. When you exist on the margins, it is easy to see the others who also exist there. They may be sitting by themselves in the cafeteria or playing alone at recess. As I got older, I played basketball on the school teams. I would periodically go home with a fellow team member and would see the abject poverty in which he lived. Though these teammates were often popular at school, they too lived on the margins.

Each community we moved to had slightly different cultural norms. The crowds I hung out with also differed. In Arkansas, my friends loved to hunt and fish. We would spend hours each day wandering through the woods or hiking through farmland to the river we were forbidden to go in. In Fort Worth, I ate lunch with a Hispanic gang and played basketball with guys affiliated with a different gang. In Florida, my friends were primarily Anglo and conservative.

In college, I thrived because everybody was new. Thanks to my childhood experiences, I knew how to make friends quickly with a wide variety of people. I began college at Samford University in Birmingham, Alabama. It was a city and state that I had traveled to on occasion to visit relatives but, overall, I had spent very little time there. In 1994, I heard a college lecture given by Samford University's legendary history professor Jim Brown. I was captivated. I had never listened to such a knowledgeable recount of history. By the time I graduated, I had taken all of Jim Brown's courses, to the benefit of my love for history but to the detriment of my GPA. Dr. Brown's mastery of his subject came with an expectation that his students would do the same. The only thing I mastered in college was the art of staying out too late!

At some point during this time, I began to wonder why I had been born into a family with so much while so many people were born into families with so little. Dr. Brown's history lectures gave me perspective on my own childhood experiences of families from very different backgrounds. Religion classes raised questions about human existence and social justice. I began asking pastors, professors, and religious leaders about wealth inequity, but nothing seemed to satisfy my troubled mind. Most of them told me I was fortunate to have grown up with much and that I should be grateful. Though their words seemed partially correct, they did not seem consistent with what I was learning about my Christian faith, human history, or life on the margins.

Turning Point

In the summer of 1997, I took a job as a youth minister in a small congregation outside Birmingham. The pastor and I hit it off in spite of the fact that we probably agreed on very little theologically and politically. I had grown up in large churches with large youth groups. We had gone on amazing trips and had activities planned for us all summer. In contrast, this church was small and so was its budget. The Birmingham kids were from working-class families and didn't have the same opportunities I had experienced in the churches of my youth.

I wanted this group of youth to have experiences with the world outside their neighborhood, similar to what I had in the congregations of my youth. So the pastor helped me negotiate a larger budget, we came up with some creative fund raisers, and we found places to stay with friends and other churches. The result was a summer packed full of trips and great experiences. I also pored over the Gospels with the youth that summer. As Baptists, so much of our time is spent on the death and resurrection of Jesus, and rightly so, but we often do this to the neglect of learning about his life. We believe that God incarnate walked this earth for thirty-three years, so I wanted the youth to know what Jesus's life was like—what he did, who he spent his time with, what he taught.

After one of the exhausting trips that summer, I sat in my dorm room planning to do something mindless. I turned on the TV to a movie that had already begun, so I didn't see what it was called. I knew that the main character's name was Francesco and, based on the picture quality and its primarily folk music soundtrack, that it had been made in the early 1970s.[1]

One of the first things I noticed was that Francesco was very popular among his friends in the community. Eventually, he decided to fight in the Crusades, was captured in battle, and was put in a Muslim prison, where he came across the Gospel of Luke. After he spent some time in prison, his father purchased his freedom, and Francesco was taken home. Though he was out of prison, he was very ill—so ill, in fact, that he fell into a coma. While in this coma, he wrestled with dreams of his past and what seemed to be a calling to the future. His father had profited greatly during the war, so Francesco woke up to a household of wealth and a father who was eager to share it with him.

But Francesco had been changed by what he had read in prison. His sights seemed set on another place. He frequently ventured beyond the city gates to watch Clare, a woman from his community, bathe lepers in the river. He was disgusted by what he saw but could not stop watching. She seemed to know something that he did not. She was modeling the love of neighbor so clearly that he instinctually knew what she was doing was inherently right, though it was also completely foreign to him.

The movie showed Francesco walking home late one evening. He came across a church in ruins and entered the dilapidated building to find a crucifix icon on the wall. He became fixated on the crucifix, and then he heard a call. The call was from God, and God was telling him to rebuild his church. Francesco broke down. In the moments following, he seemed to have great clarity that his quest for fame and possessions was keeping him from loving his neighbor. Things seemed so clear to Francesco, and he could not wait to share this new vision for life with his community and his family.

As he left the church, he crossed paths with a leper and kissed him on the lips. After he arrived home, he began giving away all of his family's possessions. Family members thought he had gone mad. His father was outraged and took Francesco to see the priest. The priest recognized that Francesco hadn't gone mad but had just had a spiritual experience, and so he could find no fault in him. Then Francesco, seeing that he had caused great pain to his father, took off his robe and handed it to his father. Robeless—completely naked—in front of a crowd that had gathered, he said, "I now no longer have an earthly father but only a heavenly Father." After this declaration, Francesco went to live a life intertwined with those on the margins—the poor and sick—to rebuild the Church of San Damiano.[2]

This was my answer to the question of inequity. I knew immediately what I needed to do. I gathered my possessions, everything that had meaning to me or that gave me status in my small world, loaded up my car, and drove to the park where the homeless spent their time. It was the same Birmingham park, Kelly Ingram Park, where Bull Conner and the Birmingham police had turned fire hoses and dogs on African American children protesting segregation and voting rights laws during the civil rights movement.[3] I got out of my car and started a conversation with a few homeless people who were congregating on a park bench. I asked if they needed anything and then offered my possessions. The hardest thing to give away was my backpacking equipment, as I loved to hike and camp. But I remember thinking that while I loved to camp, I did so only a few times a year, whereas these homeless families camped out almost every night and needed the equipment much more than I did.[4]

Following Francesco's lead, I had given away my possessions, and at that moment I knew I had been called to the poor. But I had no idea what that meant. I didn't even know that Francesco was, in fact, St. Francis of Assisi. I just knew that I was different. Something in my world had completely changed. I did not need to stand naked in the town square, but I had come to a turning point in my search for truth about the inequity of wealth and about Jesus's life, and I had found it that morning on my day off, hoping to watch some mindless TV in my dorm room.

As I continued to study Scripture, I recognized Jesus in a whole new way. I saw that he was one who forewent power and privilege, despite his gifts of knowledge, of communication, and as an organizer—not to mention the miracles. He easily could have become an earthly king, but instead he had a vision that went beyond human recognition. He spent his time with the working class, moved seamlessly in and out of the lives of sinners, healed the sick, and fed the poor and hungry. He was a man of God and of the people.[5]

After my encounter with St. Francis and my reencounter with the Jesus of the Gospels, my life gained purpose for the first time. I was able to see people as a reflection of God's image. They were an end in and of themselves and not merely a means to my greater end. I had heard people who had similar experiences say that it was as if cataracts were removed from their eyes, and they didn't even know they had spent their lives looking through them until that moment of clarity. (Paul's conversion in Acts 9:1–19, when he went literally blind until God used Ananias to restore his sight, is one prominent example.) This had become true for me too. I didn't literally go blind, but I hadn't been seeing the whole picture. Now I could see.

In the weeks following my Franciscan experience, I frequently returned to the park where I had met the homeless families. I wanted to get to know them. I quickly learned that many of them suffered from mental illness.[6] I almost learned this the hard way. One day a man in the park approached me with an antler in his hand that he had made into a shiv. He looked as if he intended to put it in the side of my neck. Hoping to catch him off guard, I asked him to tell me a little about his homemade weapon. "That is an incredible looking antler," I said. "May I see it?" Thankfully, the look of violence on his face changed, and he beamed with pride and handed it over promptly so I could look at his handiwork.

As I spent time in the park, I learned that the man I had given my backpacking equipment to had sold it for drugs within a few days.[7] I realized immediately that addressing poverty was going to be more difficult than the Hollywood version of St. Francis's story. There would be no holding hands and skipping off into the sunset in America's inner cities. Poverty is complex, and it has been present for almost all of human history. I decided the next step I needed to take was to move into an inner-city neighborhood. I knew that I needed to be immersed in the realities of poverty if I wanted to understand it. I had to learn from experience, from relationships.

The Hope House

After graduation, I was accepted into Baylor University's Truett Seminary. I moved to Texas in August 1998—a summer with fifty or more consecutive days of over 100-degree heat—in an old beat-up sedan with no air-conditioning. By the time I arrived, my left arm was deeply tan from hanging outside my window during the long drive from Virginia, where I had been living that summer.

When I began at Truett, the seminary was still new—having graduated only one class—and it felt like a family. Professors, students, and administrators spent time getting to know one another. We were eager to practice the disciplines the saints before us had put into practice, whether it was contemplative prayer, fasting, or sharing our possessions. We were learning in an academically rigorous environment and strengthening our faith simultaneously.

At an apartment I shared with a seminary classmate, students came together weekly to pray, fast, and seek discernment regarding how we might better serve the poor in our community. During those times, we came up with a vision for what we called the Hope House, which would include space in the inner city where seminary students could live, congregate, and serve the community.

As we neared the end of our first year of seminary, four of us decided to rent a house together the upcoming year. We scoured the community trying to find something we could afford, and one of the guys found a four-bedroom house that was cheaper than the apartment I was currently sharing with another student. When we visited it for the first time, it had the charm of something straight out of a Tolkien novel. The doors and porches had large archways, and there was a large living room that would be great for entertaining our friends from the seminary. It seemed perfect. Naturally, we called it Gandalf's Lair.

Living in that house taught me some important lessons. For one, I now know that there is probably a catch when you find a large home with incredibly cheap rent. Shortly after we moved in, we realized that our neighborhood was different than we previously thought. The incredibly large homes across the street didn't belong to wealthy families but were halfway houses for people getting out of prison for drug-related crimes, including murder in at least one case.

One evening I looked outside to see a number of women hanging out in our front yard. Apparently, our yard was the center of the prostitution trade in Waco. It was incredibly hot that night, so I decided to take cold water to the prostitutes outside. I made it clear that I was not interested in soliciting their services and that I was simply one of the new guys who had just moved in to the neighborhood. Once I had convinced them that I really did live there, they introduced themselves, and I met several of the women who were working that night, including Daisy and her daughter.[8]

Over the next few years of getting to know Daisy and the other women who congregated in our yard, I learned about the horrific encounters these women faced daily. It was not uncommon for us to find out that one of the women was in the hospital after being severely beaten by a john. They lived in constant fear of their pimp and the johns they solicited each evening.[9] One thing that dawned on me shortly after meeting Daisy and her daughter was that her daughter grew up knowing only prostitution as a way of survival. As we joke in my family, our family business is ministry. I was probably at seminary at least in part because that is what many of my family members, including my father and mother, had done before me. Was Daisy's daughter any different from me in that regard? Was it my place to judge Daisy's daughter for the dire situation she found herself in?

In addition to Daisy and the other women working in our front yard, we wanted to get to know the larger community. We initially tried to do this by having Bible studies on Sunday evenings and inviting our neighbors. For some odd reason, this did not work very well. People just did not want to get to know strangers by going to their home for a Bible study. (Who would've thought?) As seminary students, learning about the Bible was what we wanted to do, so we just assumed that the community would want to do so as well.

Since that failed miserably, we revised our plans. I started going across the street to play basketball with the guys at the halfway house. We set out chairs for the homeless people to sit on as they chatted throughout the day. And we continued taking cold water to the women working in the evenings in our front yard. Occasionally, we would even scrape together enough money to have our neighbors over for a cookout on our front porch.

At some point, we decided to expand our cookouts to parties for our community. We invited our seminary professors and their families, graduate students from Baylor, and people from our neighborhood. We asked everyone to bring something, even if that meant they had to panhandle for a few bucks to bring a two-liter bottle of soda. You could smell the cheap burgers and see the smoke rising up from our front yard from blocks away.

We borrowed folding chairs from a local church and scattered them throughout the yard. People from all walks of life huddled in circles sharing stories. One group laughingly traded stories about "dorm life"—a Baylor student referring to his experience at college and my neighborhood friend referring to his prison experience. We learned a lot about our friends in the community who had spent time in and out of prison.[10] Other groups at the party, consisting of seminary professors and older community members, talked about the joys and the perils that accompanied raising children. Inside the living room, music blasted as youth from the neighborhood and seminary students line danced until late in the night.

The parties were a success. Initially, between fifty and a hundred people came. By the time we had lived there a few years, sometimes a couple hundred people attended the parties. The parties worked because people from very different worlds came together in our home to talk and eat, and in so doing, they recognized their common humanity. Without even noticing it, we were living in the Hope House we had dreamed of.

James

One Saturday evening after we had lived in the house for nearly a year, I noticed a police officer parked out front. I assumed he was there to discourage prostitution and drug dealing in the neighborhood. We were planning a party for the upcoming weekend, so I decided to ask the police officer if we could block off our street and to invite him and his family to attend. I thought it might be good for him to see our community in a different light and for our community to see him as a human being, not just a badge. As I leaned over to speak with him in his car, a man drove by and shook his head at me. I didn't know the man, but my assumption was that he thought I was a snitch. A snitch, or an informant, is not a popular label in urban neighborhoods. As the familiar saying goes, "Snitches get stitches." Needless to say, I didn't want stitches.

I didn't say anything to the police officer about the man and walked back into the house and told my friends. This stopped the foosball game (appropriately located in the dining room) in its tracks. We were all nervous. For kids who had grown up in middle-class neighborhoods and suburban communities, this was a new experience. My roommates decided that I should go back outside to see if I could find the man and make peace with him. They were worried the incident could lead to a drive-by shooting and endanger the many people who tended to come over to our house. I thought their idea was a terrible suggestion, but I went anyway.

By the time I reluctantly went back outside, it was completely dark. The police officer was no longer there, and Daisy and her crew had not yet arrived. So I just sat on the curb under the lone streetlight and waited. Not long after I sat down, a male prostitute emerged from the shadows. I hadn't seen him before. He introduced himself as James[11] and he initially tried to pick me up, but as I was used to doing by that point, I made it clear I was not interested.

So James stopped making his attempts and sat down beside me. He began telling me about himself without my asking. He said he grew up being molested by the men in his life. First his father, then a stepfather, then he was moved into foster care homes where the abuse continued. James said not until he was fifteen were he and his brother moved into a foster home where they were treated like human beings and not merely objects. That was his literal language. Sadly, he said that was the last and only time in his life he could remember being treated with respect and dignity.

James's stories eventually turned from heartbreaking to hilarious. He was quite the storyteller, and he had many to tell. I finally interrupted him to see if he had seen the man I was looking for from earlier in the evening. I still had butterflies in my stomach because of that initial encounter. I wanted James to say no so I could retreat to the safety of my home and hope to never see the man again. Instead, as if on cue, James replied, "Is that him?" I looked up, and the man was walking directly toward us. I thought I was going to puke.

I nervously walked out in the middle of the street and stopped the man and introduced myself. People in the community called me Slim (a nickname I didn't particularly care for at the time but would love now). He shook my hand, and I didn't acknowledge our encounter earlier or bring up my invitation to the police officer, instead I told him about the party we were having the next week and invited him and James to come. James may have sensed my anxious energy because he launched into one of his funny stories. I am sure my discomfort was awkwardly evident, even though he had no knowledge of what had happened earlier with the police. Somehow the combination of James's stories and my invitation put the man at ease, and my tension began to dissipate. Before too long, he and I were laughing loudly together as James entertained us with his dramatic retelling of events and stories from his life. By this point, Daisy and her crew and my neighbor and his homeless cousin had joined us, and the larger James's audience became, the larger his stories became.

Time passed quickly, and it started to get late. I told the group I needed to go to bed. At the time, I was pastoring at Travis Baptist Church, a small church in rural central Texas, and I knew I needed to get some sleep. James said, "Slim, why don't you read us some Scripture?" I laughed and told him no, but I invited him to church with me the next day. He said, "No, Slim, read us some Scripture right now." I reluctantly agreed and went inside to retrieve my Bible. When I returned, I read them a passage out of Matthew:

> Therefore I tell you, do not worry about your life, what you will eat or what you will drink, or about your body, what you will wear. Is not life more than food, and the body more than clothing? Look at the birds of the air; they neither sow nor reap nor gather into barns, and yet your heavenly Father feeds them. Are you not of more value than they? And can any of you by worrying add a single hour to your span of life? And why do you worry about clothing? Consider the lilies of the field, how they grow; they neither toil nor spin, yet I tell you, even Solomon in all his glory was not clothed like one of these. But if God so clothes the grass of the field, which is alive today and tomorrow is thrown into the oven, will he not much more clothe you— you of little faith? Therefore do not worry, saying, "What will we eat?" or "What will we drink?" or "What will we wear?" For it is the Gentiles who strive for all these things; and indeed your heavenly Father knows that you need all these things. But

strive first for the kingdom of God and his righteousness, and all these things will be given to you as well.

So do not worry about tomorrow, for tomorrow will bring worries of its own. Today's trouble is enough for today. (6:25–34)

The passage was one I had gravitated to after learning more about the life of St. Francis. Ironically, it was a passage the impoverished in our community lived more faithfully than any of us attending seminary.

It had to have been after midnight by this point, but after I read the passage, James said, "Pray for us, Slim." So this group of unlikely neighbors took one another's hands, and we stood in a circle in my front yard. I stood holding the hands of a male prostitute, who hours earlier had tried to pick me up, and a man whom I had worried might commit a drive-by at our house. There we all were, Daisy and her crew, my neighbor and his homeless cousin, praying in the front yard of my house in this poor neighborhood in the middle of the night.

It felt like an out-of-body experience. I remember it as if I were looking down from above, watching the entire event take place. First, I prayed. Then James prayed. James's prayer seemed like it was taken straight from the Psalms. He prayed in earnest for his friends' safety that evening, knowing how dangerous johns can be, and he gave thanks for what they did have. I was overwhelmed with the Spirit of God in that moment.

Father Gutiérrez

Recently, I spoke with a friend who is a senior fellow at a conservative-leaning think tank. He was lamenting that there aren't more conservatives at the table in the discussion of national poverty issues. I explained that this is because conservatives have largely been blaming the poor for their plight rather than identifying ways to strengthen the ladder of economic opportunity for all Americans. Though he and his colleagues in Washington, DC, are trying to change this type of discourse, he disagreed with my assessment and made a valuable point. He pointed out that conservatives often provide valuable support to people in poverty through local nonprofit organizations and faith communities, and he was correct. There are many "compassionate conservatives" (to borrow a term popularized by President George W. Bush) who are addressing hunger and poverty in our world.[12] I will discuss the success of this methodology later in this book, and their role in this issue is undeniable.

Just as my friend didn't see conservatives at the table, as a seminary student I didn't encounter any conservative theologians who claimed we are responsible for the poor. Rather, I encountered liberation theologians. One in particular was Father Gustavo Gutiérrez, who is widely considered the "father of liberation theology."[13] Father Gutiérrez operates from the mind-set that God has a preference for the poor and thus believes we should as well. He spent much of his life as a priest living and working among the poor in Lima, Peru. According to Father Gutiérrez, "If there is no friendship with [the poor] and no sharing of the life of the poor, then there is no authentic commitment to liberation, because love exists only among equals."[14] His lifelong friendship with and work among the poor began to give me a biblical and theological framework for my work among people in poverty.

While still at Truett, I found out that Father Gutiérrez was planning to visit Baylor, and one of our faculty members, whom he had befriended, was going to have him over to his home to celebrate the priest's birthday. I was among several students who were invited to join them. We gathered around the professor's kitchen table to sing "Happy Birthday" to Father Gutiérrez, he blew out the candles, and we ate together. Several of my more outgoing and assertive classmates sat next to him at the table and peppered him with questions for much of the evening. Admittedly, I was too shy and nervous to get in a word. I just sat back and watched and listened to this man—a giant in my mind and in the formation of my life—answer questions with gentleness and humility. He was not at all what I had imagined. This theological giant ironically has a very short build; I have described him to my friends as a Peruvian Yoda. Moreover, while his books were written with a fiery temper and prophetic judgment, in person he was a kind, compassionate, and gentle older man.

As we began transitioning to the living room, he and I got up from the table at the same time and were walking through the kitchen together. I knew that if I was ever going to get the courage to speak to him, this would be my chance. I turned toward him, hunched over, and asked him a question that had been on my mind since moving into the 15th Street home several years prior: "How does one have solidarity with the poor?"

He looked into my eyes and said, "Commit your life to their cause."

His wisdom cut through me like a knife. As Baptists, we baptize by immersion. We say, "Buried with Christ in baptism and raised to walk in a new life." Those early years certainly felt like I was being immersed and raised into a new life. Father Gutiérrez had given me my commission, and my unlikely circle of neighbors out in front of the Hope House baptized me into it.

These experiences became a foundation for my life to come and frame much of my understanding of poverty today. I am grateful for the lessons and, more important, for the people who taught me during those early formative years. I hope today and in the years to come to put those lessons into practice.

THE PEOPLE

Finding Citizenship in the Right Kingdom

The American Southwest

In 2014, Congress established the National Commission on Hunger, a bipartisan ten-member commission created to find ways the US can more effectively and efficiently address the issue of hunger. I was lucky enough to be appointed to this commission. In order to best understand the issue, the commission traveled to communities across the country to hear directly from the people. One trip took us to the American Southwest. We visited tribal lands in southern New Mexico and desert communities along the Texas-Mexico border. The trip was in the early summer, the desert sun was already hot, and traveling across the region on a small tour bus was exhausting. As we went from community to community, listening to stories, we heard from committed individuals and organizations addressing the food needs of their communities in creative ways. We also heard heartbreaking stories of hunger and poverty and their spiraling effects on families simply trying to make enough money to get by each week.

The last few days of our trip took us to the city of El Paso, Texas, directly on the border with Mexico. There we sat down with a group of elders from the community who had met one another in a citizenship class they were taking at the La Fe Community Center in downtown El Paso. Most of them had lived in the United States their entire lives and had raised their children here. Many of these children had enlisted to serve in the military and were in the Middle East on active duty as we spoke. These undocumented elders were not rapists or drug smugglers. They had been business owners, welders, and car mechanics, and their one wish was to die as citizens of the country where they had spent much of their lives.

The elders had another thing in common: they were all regularly experiencing hunger. Almost all the men had been injured on jobs but received no worker's compensation because they were not US citizens. The women had worked throughout their childhood as laborers in fields, then as adults in hotels as custodial staff—jobs that did not include retirement benefits. Toward the end of our conversation, I asked them pointedly, "Do you have any food to eat?" Hearing this question, one proud elderly man with a chiseled chin and a pointed mustache simply buried his head in his hands and began to weep. His wife sat up, straightened her dress, and then spoke. "Occasionally we are able to put food on the table. When we do, it is normally one meal a day. I will make us a plate of beans and a couple of tortillas. We are older, so we don't need as much."

The rest of the group had avoided eye contact with me when I had asked the question, hoping I would not call on them. But when the elderly woman spoke, they listened intently and nodded in agreement as if she were speaking for all of them. At that point, one of the men looked up, wiped his tears, and said, "Remember us when you come into your kingdom."

I immediately had to excuse myself to find a private place. I went down an empty hall, pushed my way into a bathroom, and wept.

My home congregation regularly sings a Taizé chant that quotes the robber on the cross next to Jesus saying, "Jesus, remember me when you come into your kingdom." We sing the line over and over again.

As many times as I had sung that song or read those words, I had never imagined myself living in a kingdom now. I had always thought about the passage only in regard to Jesus creating the kingdom of heaven on earth in the future. This man's comment flipped these words with which I was so familiar. After all, he was preparing to leave our discussion and go back to the isolation many elderly people in our nation experience daily, to a home with very little food. I would leave and return to a nice hotel, eat a nice meal, then go to the halls of power in Washington to deliver our report.

"Remember us when you come into your kingdom."

The following day we climbed out of our bus and made our way into the La Fe Community Center to hear public testimony. We were guided into a large, empty auditorium and took our seats at a row of tables elevated on a stage. We would be looking down at individuals who would stand before us as if they were testifying before a panel of judges. The room soon began to fill, and we called our first of over a dozen people invited to speak. We were scheduled to hear nearly ten hours of testimony— several hours of specific individuals invited to speak and then several hours of public testimony from anyone who wanted to have their voice heard.

Quite a few hours in, Dr. Joe Sharkey, a professor leading a public health research project in the *colonías* on the border, took his seat at the table below the stage to tell us about his experience addressing hunger and health. He began by telling us the story of one of his public health workers, Linda,[1] and her visit to homes in the *colonías*.

If you are not familiar with the *colonías*, it may be difficult for you to grasp the living conditions they present. These particular *colonías* in west Texas sit on the far edges of the city, sprawling in the middle of the desert. Often, they do not have running water or electricity, much less paved roads. Homes in the *colonías* tend to be built with the materials at hand, and it is not uncommon to see a one-room home with one wall made of corrugated metal, another of plywood, and another of rocks salvaged from the surrounding land. Property in the *colonías* is typically not owned by the residents but is leased from landowners who may *come and take it* whenever they please. We do not often think of people in the US living in conditions such as these, but in the *colonías* of rural border towns, they are normal.

Dr. Sharkey explained to us that public health workers like Linda use a simple set of questions to check on the health and well-being of the community members they are visiting. He went on to tell us about one of Linda's visits to a community member named Maria. After brief introductions, Linda began asking questions regarding the health of Maria's family. For her final question, Linda asked, "Maria, do you have any food in the house?" Hearing the question, Maria's head slowly lowered under the weight of shame and guilt, which sounded similar to the countenance of the elders the day prior. Without saying a word, Maria guided Linda to her kitchen and pointed to a small refrigerator. (Maria lived in a *colonía* that occasionally had electricity.) Linda opened it and saw that it was completely empty except for one little bag of chicken bones. Puzzled, Linda asked Maria, "Why is there a bag of chicken bones inside your fridge?"

Through tears, Maria responded, "So when my children open the refrigerator door, they will at least see that something is in there."

In my work in Texas, I have visited many homes in the *colonías* across the border region. I have met many women like Maria and interacted with many children living in similar situations.

Listening to Dr. Sharkey, I just kept thinking that surely we can do better than this.

Our commission was sent across the country to try to identify the root causes of hunger and to find out what we can do as a nation to improve lives. What we discovered was not a surprise. For most people, their lack of access to food was a direct result of their lack of access to money. However, their lack of access to money was often contextual. For the people in the desert, their lack of citizenship resulted in low wages, which kept them food insecure.

"Remember us when you come into your kingdom."

Regretfully, we have not remembered our brothers and sisters: 39.7 million people in the US live in poverty,[2] 12.8 million of them are children[3] and 4.7 million are senior adults;[4] 41.2 million Americans are considered food insecure;[5] 12.9 million children live in food-insecure households;[6] and every county in the US has reported food insecurity among a percentage of its population.[7]

Understanding Hunger in the US

We all have preconceived notions about people who live in poverty. It is impossible to watch the news, read a newspaper, or scan Facebook without developing a bias for or against people experiencing hunger and poverty. But let's be honest with one another: our opinions are only partially informed by Scripture. Most often they are informed by one anecdotal encounter and rarely, if ever, by reliable research. I often hear excuses from people who inform me that they have compassion for the poor in developing countries, but poor Americans must simply be lazy because we live in a land of opportunity.

Scripture is clear on the subject: feed the hungry and you will live. So what can research tell us about the hungry in the US?

In the US, certain populations bear the burdens of hunger and poverty more than others. They are senior adults, single-parent families with young children,[8] people with disabilities,[9] American Indians,[10] people with family members in the prison system,[11] immigrants,[12] people experiencing declines in mental and physical health,[13] and minority households.[14]

Hunger in our nation is primarily episodic,[15] meaning that people who experience hunger may not experience it daily. Exhausting food budgets is more common at the end of the month and may be a predictor of further health inequities.[16] The term *food insecure* is the technical term used when describing hunger. It is defined as "a lack of access to enough healthy food to live a healthy lifestyle."[17] When I served on the commission, we used the term *very low food security*—meaning someone whose food intake was reduced because of a lack of resources for food[18]—interchangeably with the word *hunger*. People experience hunger in our nation for a variety of reasons, including the following.

Underemployment

The first and most prevalent reason for hunger is underemployment. Basically, this means that many people who are experiencing hunger have jobs and are working, but their jobs don't pay enough to cover all of their living expenses—even when they are putting together as many jobs as they can find to try to make ends meet.[19] While living in San Antonio, our neighbors would often find minimum-wage jobs in the hospitality industry catering to vacationers. They would supplement those jobs with additional employment at fast-food restaurants, convenience stores, or anything else they could find.

Our neighbor Juanita lived in a duplex next door to us.[20] Her husband suffered from kidney disease and had to walk to the dialysis clinic a mile away from their home every day. Juanita was legally blind, so the city bus for the disabled population would arrive shortly after 5 a.m. to take her to the Lighthouse for the Blind, where she worked. She and her blind coworkers made army fatigues for the troops in Iraq. When her shift was over, she would catch the same bus and return home each evening at 6 p.m. On weekends, she would use her walking stick to find her way down the street to one of the local restaurants, where she would sweep the floors for extra cash.

In her testimony to the National Commission on Hunger, Donna Yellen, from the Preble Street organization in Maine, put it this way: "We hear every day loud and clear from all areas of the state that people can't support their families. They can't get food because they can't find decent jobs. The forest industry, the fishing industry, canning, textile, manufacturing are all in distress. Giant mills: empty. A major naval air station: closed. Mill towns have struggling economies. We hear about the problem of people living isolated from job centers in a state with virtually no public transportation, or the lack of affordable housing."[21]

The rise of the global economy has made it cheaper to manufacture in other countries around the globe most of what we wear, drive, plug in, and even eat. This has made finding gainful employment increasingly difficult for America's poor.

A Lack of Education

A second reason people experience hunger in our nation is directly tied to educational achievement. Simply put, a person must graduate from high school and get an additional degree to avoid hunger and poverty in the twenty-first century. Regardless of whether the degree is a technical-training degree, a two-year college degree, or a four-year college degree, for the best chance at gainful employment within our current economic climate, a person must obtain one of these.

The relationship between hunger and education can quickly become a vicious cycle. A person needs to have an education in order to have the best chance of not living in poverty, but living in poverty is a detriment to getting an education. Some of the most important predictors of whether a person will graduate from high school are reading level at third grade, family poverty, family structure, and concentrated poverty at the neighborhood level.[22] Hunger often contributes to higher dropout rates, grade repetition, and special education.[23] There are always exceptions, but if a person is not the exception, his or her chances of living in poverty and experiencing hunger increase dramatically with a lack of educational attainment.

Family Structure

Family structure is another reason individuals experience hunger. My wife, Amy, and I have three wonderful boys who are all blessings. We know how hard raising children can be and have struggled to balance our careers, our children's extracurricular activities, attending church, and so forth. We also know the financial struggle of trying to make enough to pay down debt, afford a home, make car payments, and so forth. As hard as that may be at times for us, the deck is not stacked against us. It is just the opposite. We are white. We are Christian. We both come from well-educated, middle-class households. We have numerous graduate degrees, strong social networks, and each other to lean on. We have every enviable opportunity at our disposal. Even still, raising our children can be an overwhelming challenge at times.

Being a single parent working a full-time job and raising children must be an incredibly tough prospect. Who takes the kids to school? You. Who makes dinner? You. Who works all day to pay for everything you need and then some? You. Add wanting to improve your economic condition by going back to school, as many single parents do, and you have to be superhuman to manage it all.

"The hunger rate among households headed by a single mother is four times the rate for households headed by a married couple . . . and twice that for households headed by a single father."[24] Naturally, households with one wage earner are likely to earn less than households with two wage earners, which only magnifies difficulties for those already in impoverished households, particularly women, who currently are paid 82 percent of what their male counterparts are paid.[25]

Race and Hunger

Race plays a major role in high rates of hunger in our nation, exacerbating the reasons listed so far. People of color are more likely to experience hunger in our nation.[26] Whether we want to admit it or not, we have not healed our wounds of racism. We have had our moments of triage—the abolition of slavery and the civil rights movement—which were critical steps to stop the hemorrhaging flow of racist hatred, bigotry, and indifference that were pervasive in our history. But we have not taken steps toward healing on a national level. We did not commit to reparations or put together a Truth and Reconciliation Commission, as South Africa did following apartheid. We have not integrated our neighborhoods, churches, and social groups. As a result, people in minority households are twice as likely to experience food insecurity and poverty than those in Anglo (white) households.

Aging and a Decline in Mental Health

Several years ago, prior to their passing, my grandparents were still living in their home in Springhill, Louisiana. My grandfather, a retired pastor, was beloved in the community, as was my grandmother. They were certainly two people who lived the faithful life according to Jesus's standards. But in this late stage of their lives, their mental health was deteriorating because of dementia. They would forget to do basic things, and, unfortunately, eating was one of those things. One day during an appointment, their doctor, a friend of the family, figured out that they were regularly missing meals. Through conversations with them, he also found out that on the occasions when they did remember to eat, they would drive to Sonic for a corn dog. This was unnerving for our family to hear for three reasons:

one, they were not eating regularly; two, when they were eating, it was not food with high nutritional value; and three, they were driving when they probably should not have been behind the wheel of a car.

What is alarming about this story is that my grandparents were the matriarch and patriarch of this small Louisiana town, yet they were going hungry because of their decline in mental health. Fortunately for them, once we learned of their situation, my aunts and uncles and my grandparents' church sprang into action to ensure that they were provided for through a Meals on Wheels program with daily check-ins. Imagine what would have happened to them if they had not had family, health insurance, or a strong social network.

I am asked frequently by people in congregations what they should do to address food needs in their local communities. My first question back to them is, "Are you participating in a senior meals program?" Since every county in the country has hunger, every church in the country should at the very least partner with a Meals on Wheels program. Not only do such programs provide meals to seniors who may not otherwise have food, but they also provide a human connection to people who may not get that regularly, if ever. Furthermore, since federal funds have ironically been cut for such a vital program while our elderly population is exploding, churches need to put these programs into their budgets.

The Need to Make Trade-offs

People experiencing hunger are forced to make trade-offs each month. They are forced to decide whether to pay their rent, their medical bills, their car payment, their child care costs, their electricity bill, or to buy food. Food is often the one negotiable item. If people don't pay their electricity bill, their power is shut off. If they don't pay their rent, they are kicked out of their home. If their car payment goes unpaid, their car is repossessed. But if they don't buy food, they will just be hungry. Yes, not having food leads to less productivity at work and school, increases mental health decline, and causes shame, but they get to keep their home.

These, of course, are not all the root causes of hunger, but they are some of the most prevalent. Other key contributors include exposure to violence, immigration status, housing instability, incarceration, and medical debt. Naturally, much has been made of people who do not take personal responsibility for themselves and are thus hungry and living in poverty. Obviously, "individuals make many life choices that can affect financial circumstances and hunger: choices about staying in or dropping out of high school, choices about getting a job or not, and choices about having or delaying children."[27] Taking personal responsibility for oneself and one's family must occur for any intervention to work. Not taking personal responsibility is certainly a problem, but it is much less of one than we have been led to believe. From my two decades of living and working in impoverished conditions, I can affirm that these people do exist, but they are the exception.

The Sheep and the (Scape) Goats

Scapegoating has been a literal practice for thousands of years, with the concept originating in Leviticus 16:7–10. In Old Testament times, a goat was designated to take on the sins of the community and then was cast out into the desert to die. In so doing, the community members rid themselves of their sins and could go on with life as they knew it. They repeated the scapegoating practice each year on the Day of Atonement. Later, the ancient Greeks stepped the practice up a level and would cast out a paraplegic or a beggar as a response to a famine, a plague, or an invasion of some kind. Casting out this person cleared the larger society of its debts and let the people move on with life without having to reckon with any true causes of their situation.

As we like to do, Americans have one-upped the Greeks. We have scapegoated not one animal or even just one person; we have cast out an entire socioeconomic class of people. Our economic hardships are not evenly dispersed throughout society. Rather, the same families that struggle with bouts of hunger also do not have affordable health care. These same families send their children to schools where graduation rates are well below 50 percent and college readiness is in the single digits. They are also the same families that have lacked livable wage-paying jobs for generations. They are our scapegoats sent to live in deserted urban neighborhoods and the rural mobile home parks we avoid. We literally have paved our roads and interstates so we can circumvent neighborhoods full of our scapegoats and can avoid being confronted with the way our own selfishness has been cast on the impoverished so we can go on with our lives.

To scapegoat and push the poor out of our minds, we have had to dehumanize them. We have worked hard to classify the poor as lazy, to divide them as deserving and undeserving. We have developed theologies of prosperity to lift those who are rich in order to demonize those who are poor. Thus, it becomes morally defensible for some children to have an abundance of food while others have a bag of chicken bones in the fridge. We can just blame the parent for being lazy or an illegal.

We have created the myth of the welfare queen. According to this myth, the welfare queen, living off government programs, drives a Cadillac, owns an iPhone and a big-screen TV, and eats lobster paid for by food stamps funded by hardworking American taxpayers who receive no such benefits from the overreaching federal government. We make the welfare queen, rather than people like my neighbor Juanita, emblematic of all people in poverty. The welfare queen is completely undeserving of compassion and is a construct of her own making. This justifies our casting her out into the wilderness—the deserted place where only death lingers.

As a culture, this dehumanization has become our standard rhetoric—Christian and non-Christian alike. We are guilty of engaging in the generational process of dehumanizing the poor.[28] Either we actively employ language and images to solidify these beliefs and attitudes or we perpetuate dehumanization because of a lack of awareness and critical consciousness. Basically, we choose not to see it. This too is an implicit bias that we must name and overcome.[29] If we don't recognize the ways systems are stacked against the poor (even when they are aggressively created to do so), we are also complicit in scapegoating.[30] Scapegoating, therefore, can be both intentionally aggressive and unintentionally passive.

Regardless, this practice is antithetical to what we read in Matthew 25:34–36: "Come, you that are blessed by my Father, inherit the kingdom prepared for you from the foundation of the world; for I was hungry and you gave me food, I was thirsty and you gave me something to drink, I was a stranger and you welcomed me, I was naked and you gave me clothing, I was sick and you took care of me, I was in prison and you visited me."

The goats that are cast out in Matthew are those who did *not* give food to the hungry, the ones who did *not* provide shelter for the stranger or clothing for the naked. Matthew calls us not only to see the hungry as humans but also to see the hungry as Jesus.[31]

5

THE DESERT

Moving from Mind-Sets
of Scarcity to Abundance

On their return the apostles told Jesus all they had done. He took them with him and withdrew privately to a city called Bethsaida. When the crowds found out about it, they followed him; and he welcomed them, and spoke to them about the kingdom of God, and healed those who needed to be cured.

The day was drawing to a close, and the twelve came to him and said, "Send the crowd away, so that they may go into the surrounding villages and countryside, to lodge and get provisions; for we are here in a deserted place." But he said to them, "You give them something to eat." They said, "We have no more than five loaves and two fish—unless we are to go and buy food for all these people." For there were about five thousand men. And he said to his disciples, "Make them sit down in groups of about fifty each." They did so and made them all sit down. And taking the five loaves and the two fish, he looked up to heaven, and blessed and broke them, and gave them to the disciples to set before the crowd. And all ate and were filled. What was left over was gathered up, twelve baskets of broken pieces.

—Luke 9:10–17

You Give Them Something to Eat!

The disciples have just returned from their first mission trip without Jesus. He had sent seventy-two of them across Israel to heal the sick and preach about the kingdom of God. They witnessed and performed miracles and undoubtedly felt God move through them in ways they could not ever have imagined. Now the mission trip is over. All they want to do is tell Jesus everything.

I can imagine Peter with the entire group of disciples excitedly coming up to Jesus in the middle of a crowd in an urban area and saying, "Let's go to our favorite desert camping spot [I am imagining Big Bend in Texas]. Our mission trip was ahmazing! Really transformational!"

Jesus probably laughed at their eagerness and said, "Let's do it!"

So they try to sneak away with Jesus in order to have some private time with him. But they likely forgot: there are seventy-two of them! If you have ever been with a youth group returning from a great mission trip, you know that nothing they do is either quiet or stealthy. Imagine a group of seventy-two of them.

By the time they get to the desert, thousands of people have followed them. Jesus is the rock star of this community, and everyone wants to see and hear what is next. So Jesus begins to teach the crowd and heal the sick. Then the eagerness of the disciples likely turns into resentment. (Obviously, I was not there, but that is how I read the text.)

Peter probably told Matthew and John, "These people are ruining our favorite place to camp." John may have responded,

"I bet they just want a handout from Jesus." Then Matthew probably chimes in, "Don't they have jobs? Why aren't they working right now? They are so lazy! They don't deserve Jesus's help." So the seventy-two disciples just sit together brooding.

This continues all day long, and it is getting dark. Jesus has been teaching the crowd and healing their sick, and the disciples have had enough of it. So Peter and his leadership team boldly walk over to Jesus. "Jesus, enough is enough! Send everyone home. You were supposed to hang out with us, not them. Besides, we don't have a place for these people to stay or any food for them."

Jesus, who is likely ministering to someone while Peter complains, responds, "You give them something to eat."

Peter says, "But Jesus, we are in the desert, and all we have are two fish and five loaves of bread for five thousand people!"

Jesus nonchalantly responds, "That'll work. Sit everybody down, and let's get this buffet started."

The disciples have just witnessed Jesus healing the sick, and they have heard him teach about the kingdom of God, but when they are in a deserted place, they immediately resort to an ideology of personal responsibility. Yet this is perpetually when God moves throughout human history. When we have exhausted almost all resources—when we are in a deserted place—that is when miracles happen.

When the disciples see desert, Jesus sees opportunity. When we see scarcity, Jesus shows us the way of abundance. Jesus often sees resources and scalable solutions when his disciples see only barren wilderness. That is why Jesus's witness has inspired revolutionary acts of loving-kindness and resourcefulness for two thousand years. He ushered in an upside-down kingdom where the faithful like St. Francis of Assisi leave the safety and the security of the kingdoms of their world to join the outsiders—the immigrants, the poor, the hungry, the mentally ill—resulting in a peaceable kingdom built on a foundation of justice.

Food Deserts

Twenty years ago, when my seminary friends and I moved into a house in inner-city Waco, I met Jimmy and Janet Dorrell. It turns out Jimmy and Janet had decided to move out of their kingdoms and live among the poor long before I had even heard of St. Francis, much less decided to follow his lead. After attending Baylor and getting jobs, the Dorrells decided to relocate to a deserted urban neighborhood, where they eventually started Mission Waco, an organization dedicated to empowering the poor and marginalized in Waco. Prior to meeting the Dorrells, I had no idea that people lived in and worked to serve impoverished communities. Jimmy opened a new world to me. He helped me understand my calling and trained me in the art of Christian community development, to see assets in communities where most people see only blight or danger. Jimmy did the best he could to teach me how to talk about justice for the poor with the powerful and the affluent. Admittedly, my self-righteous indignation (which I refer to as my spiritual gift, along with yelling at referees) made the latter lesson one I did not learn easily.

Recently, Mission Waco was able to acquire a large, empty building in its neighborhood, and, staying true to its core values, the organization asked the people in the neighborhood what they wanted to do with it. While there were a variety of answers, some more feasible than others, one common thread was that the neighborhood wanted a grocery store. The neighborhood Mission Waco is in is a food desert. If you're not familiar with that term, food deserts are areas, often urban poor areas or rural areas, where people do not have access to healthy food because there are no grocery stores or healthy food providers (much less farmers markets).[1] The only food sources are likely fast-food restaurants or convenience stores. The result is hunger and obesity—two seemingly disparate issues going hand in hand. When people do not have transportation to distant grocery stores, they either do not eat regularly or are forced to buy food that is close and cheap, making junk food a large part of their diets. Ironically, people with inconsistent access to food frequently experience diet-related diseases thought to be a result of having too much food.

Once Mission Waco and the community decided on a grocery store, they got to work. Donations were raised, the building was renovated, and they even planted vegetables and installed an aquaponics system. The process took time, but eventually an empty building was transformed into a grocery store, and a neighborhood was no longer a food desert. The name of the new nonprofit grocery store is Jubilee Market.

Rather than spending his energy scapegoating the poor, Jimmy is spending his life on behalf of the hungry. He is one person among a chorus of people transforming their communities by seeing in desolation opportunities for justice.

What is unique about the poverty-related issue of hunger is the amount of resources available to address the issue. That is in part why I call hunger the broken streetlight of poverty-related issues. Though there are millions of food-insecure Americans, there are also strong federal nutrition programs run primarily by the United States Department of Agriculture (USDA)— many of which support farmers and grocers. There are corporations, foundations, and congregations, all with funding allocated to provide food for the hungry. When these resources are paired with creative, community-minded families like the Dorrells, miracles happen in deserted places.

School Breakfast

Shortly after the launch of the Texas Hunger Initiative (THI) in the spring of 2009, I began to immerse myself in learning about the resources available to us and the needs going unaddressed. In that initial assessment, I learned of a brain development study done by several Baylor faculty members to understand the effects of stress on children in high-poverty communities.

They learned that infants and toddlers who grow up in highly stressful, ever-changing environments—where food or consistent places to sleep may not be certainties—can struggle to think in patterns. Simply put, the children were unable to understand that two always follows one or that B always follows A, because consistent patterns were not a part of their realities. So when these children start kindergarten, they are unable to count and learn the alphabet, much less learn to read.[2]

I knew that not having breakfast in the morning could inhibit students' focus and impede their learning, but it was eye-opening to realize that not having consistent access to basic necessities could have such an impact on fundamental brain development and place students at a disadvantage from the moment they began their education. Add to that what we know regarding high school graduation rates and reading on a third-grade level and it's not hard to see that many children's fates were basically sealed at birth. I am not a neuroscientist, but this seems to agree with Maslow's hierarchy of needs.[3]

I visited schools across Texas where teachers told me that the number one question they got each morning was, "Is it almost lunchtime?" So our already underpaid, overworked teachers paid for snacks out of their own pockets to give to students who were hungry and distracted because they hadn't eaten breakfast that morning—and maybe hadn't eaten dinner the night before. It would be one thing if there simply was not enough food for all the students to have three meals a day, but the problem was that the resources available were being significantly underutilized. One such resource was the School Breakfast Program. In Texas, 3.1 million students participated in the National School Lunch Program, receiving a free or reduced-price lunch every day in 2009.[4] These same students were eligible to receive breakfast at school, but only a fraction of them did.

To better understand why children were not getting breakfast at school, THI's Kathy Krey and Erin Nolen led research efforts to study the academic and nutritional benefits of school breakfast, specifically universal breakfast in the classroom.[5] They discovered that children in high poverty communities who ate breakfast at school performed better academically, consumed more nutrients, and had fewer discipline problems.[6] Additionally, they learned that when breakfast was offered to all children in their classrooms, after the school day began, doing so doubled participation and reduced the stigma of being a poor kid eating in the cafeteria before school.[7] Naturally, we shared this research with school districts across Texas, prompting many to evaluate their breakfast programs and make changes to increase participation. As a result of the collective work of our research team, field staff, and schools across the state, 390 million additional breakfasts were served to children between 2009 and 2017.[8]

In most cases, we encountered principals, teachers, and school district administrators who were simply unaware that this underutilized resource could yield profound results simply by changing the location where breakfast was offered.

Now when I visit schools, I hear some very different stories. One teacher, Lisa,[9] admitted apprehension about giving up fifteen minutes of her academic time for breakfast in the classroom, especially with the rising pressures of standardized testing. She reluctantly went along with her principal's requirement and soon found a creative way to maximize breakfast time with her students. "My father always looked so smart and sophisticated when he would sit at the table and read the paper, drink his coffee, and eat breakfast," she told me. "He would engage us in conversations about what was happening in the world, and I would leave for school well fed and already mentally stimulated."[10]

Lisa decided to create this same atmosphere in her classroom. "I call breakfast time our 'family meal.' I decided to get copies of *Time Magazine for Kids* and have the students read articles as they eat their breakfast. I ask them questions about the articles they are reading. We have delightful conversations about the world, and my students never realize they are doing reading comprehension work."[11]

At another school, the principal told me how she decided to use breakfast in the classroom as a leadership development opportunity for her students. She created a program in which students take breakfast carts to each classroom and provide meals for their peers. The opportunity was advertised as being a select, important duty, and students flocked to apply. To be chosen for the role, students submitted résumés to their teachers and had to interview with the school principal. If they were chosen for the honorable role, they had to be at school on time, do well academically, and be role models for their peers.[12]

Seeing the changes in school breakfast participation reminds me of Jesus seeing his disciples fishing but catching no fish and then telling them to cast their nets on the other side of their boats. They did, and after that simple change, their haul was so large they could barely get it back to shore (see John 21:3–6). When schools simply change the location of breakfast, participation rates often increase from 30 percent to 90 percent.

Summer Hunger

Families in poverty struggle to pay for food throughout the school year, even when they can count on schools to provide some food for their children. Add several additional mouths to feed during the summer, and families are sunk financially. After all, their employers are not giving them a summer raise to pay for the extra meals needed.

My coworker Doug experienced this early in his career. Doug was a school social worker assigned to mentor at-risk youth. One of his students, a high school junior named Michael,[13] thrived under Doug's mentorship. His grades improved, he came to school on time, and he had fewer discipline problems as the year progressed. Obviously, Doug was proud of the work Michael was doing and of his own efforts to intervene in Michael's life, but as summer approached, Michael's grades began to decline, and he started getting in trouble again. One afternoon Doug pulled him aside, exasperated, and asked him, "What is going on? You were doing so well!"

Michael responded, "I'm sorry, Doug, but summer is coming up, and I know that if I get sent to summer school, then I'll at least get one meal a day."

Doug was stunned. The student he had poured so much into was being forced to trade his education for food, his long-term well-being for an immediate basic need.

Unfortunately, this problem is not unique to Michael or to the children Dan Trevino found in the dumpster in his church parking lot. One out of six children in America faces hunger—one out of two in south Texas. This is why the USDA's Summer Meals Program is so important. Free summer meals can be a lifeline for families in poverty, but fewer than one out of five students who eats a free or reduced-price meal at school eats a meal at a summer meals site, and so a vital and helpful resource again goes underutilized.

The Dallas community decided to do something about this for its students. Led by several nonprofit leaders, THI child hunger specialist Loretta Landry, and Share Our Strength's No Kid Hungry Campaign, they identified the children in their community who were going without meals during the summer months. Then this newly formed coalition convened every organization already addressing summer hunger or willing to do so in the future. The group developed a strategic plan that identified who would make the meals, who would serve meals, and which community organizations would become summer meal sites for the Dallas community.

But they didn't stop there. Loretta and her team created the Excellence in Summer Meals Campaign to reward organizations for serving healthy meals, providing games for the children to exercise their bodies, and offering educational activities to exercise their minds. In the first year of the campaign, five program sponsors participated in the program. No sponsors were recognized that year because the quality of food and programming did not meet the standards set by the coalition. I could tell the directors were embarrassed by the results. Fortunately, the sponsors' competitive natures kicked in for the good of their community, and they all began upping their game. They started providing increasingly healthy meals, they looked for ways to engage students academically, and they created opportunities for children to play games to keep their bodies moving. In 2019, twenty-three sponsoring organizations received recognition. Eleven of them were awarded gold status—the highest award the campaign offers—thanks to their superb food quality, educational programming, and marketing.

One school nutrition director proudly told me that when they realized how many children were missing meals in their district, they decided to offer three meals a day to them. They also keep schools open on weekends and during Christmas and spring break so kids have a place to go and have a meal. The district serves over three hundred thousand meals a day to the kids of the community. After receiving the gold standard at the 2019 awards ceremony, the nutrition director asked me, "Can we go for platinum next year?"

Trickle-up Economics

Shortly before his assassination in 1963, President John F. Kennedy proposed expanding and making permanent a small government pilot program to address domestic hunger, called the Food Stamps Program. Unfortunately, he did not live to see its passage, but President Johnson carried it through, passing the Food Stamp Act of 1964.[14] This is widely seen as the beginning of Johnson's War on Poverty.

Today the program is called the Supplemental Nutrition Assistance Program, or SNAP. SNAP is the largest federal nutrition assistance program, so naturally it comes under constant heat from the left and the right. The left wants it expanded, while the right blames it for everything from increasing the national debt to rampant fraud, and I am sure there is someone in Washington who insists that SNAP is the root cause of tensions with North Korea.

During one of our commission hearings in Portland, Maine, we heard from a SNAP recipient, Thomas Ptacek. Thomas is a military veteran who experienced homelessness. "It was not a quick and easy road back for me [from war], and the SNAP program was a big part of my success in returning to a more fulfilling life," Thomas told us. "To me, the most beneficial aspect of the SNAP program is that it allows for choice in the purchase of food that can be prepared in the home. . . . This extra piece, that I personally benefited from greatly, is the sense of normalcy and stability that comes from going to the grocery store and choosing your food."[15]

Partisanship aside, the SNAP program provides money to families living below 135 percent of the poverty level (about $33,000 for a family of four) to purchase food. States can choose to increase eligibility for families up to 165 percent of the poverty level. The amount a family receives is based on the Thrifty Food Plan, a complex formula based on current costs of food, the Consumer Price Index, and net income. If a family has a very low wage, does not own their home, has no savings, and has a car worth very little, they can get up to $600 a month in supplemental nutrition assistance. The average family benefit is around $450 per month, but some individuals may receive less than $20 a month based on income. SNAP funds are typically loaded onto an EBT card (electronic benefits card resembling a debit card) and can be used only for food in stores approved by the USDA.

In 2013, at the peak of the recession, our nation spent nearly $80 billion on the program, providing food for more than 47.6 million people. In 2017, our nation spent $68 billion on the program, providing food for 42 million people.[16] The $12 billion decline is due to the way the program was established. SNAP was set up to rise and fall with need. After the recession of 2009, it became a widely needed program and enrollment increased, but as the economy strengthened and people moved back into the workforce, the need decreased, and so did the amount spent on the program. So for haters of the program who decry the number of SNAP recipients, the message is clear: if we improve the economic well-being of all Americans, thereby reducing the need for the program, the program will naturally reduce in size.

I would love to see the day when we no longer need SNAP, but until that day, I will continue to point to the benefits of SNAP as a work support program and to the way it's working. Expanding SNAP benefits can have an economic stimulating effect. Every $1 that comes into a community through the program bolsters the Gross Domestic Product by $1.79.[17] SNAP not only provides a lot of suppers for people like veteran Thomas Ptacek but also promotes what I call *trickle-up* economics. SNAP is an investment in impoverished families, most of whom are working and contributing to the economy but are underemployed. These individuals immediately reinvest SNAP dollars by buying food at grocery stores, thus creating food sector jobs for people in grocery stores, in supply chains, and on farms and completing the circle of providing employment and economic growth in communities where they are desperately needed.

Hunger and Health

World Hunger Relief Inc. in Waco—affectionately referred to by locals as simply "the farm"—was established more than forty years ago to train missionaries and community developers to address global hunger through agriculture. People come from around the world to this small farm in central Texas to learn sustainable ways to grow crops and raise livestock for the purpose of empowering the global community to reduce hunger and poverty. (Amy and I did internships at the farm before our children were born.)

In 2017, the farm committed not only to educate the global community about reducing hunger through sustainable agriculture but also to embark on a program to get the food it grows to food-insecure families in central Texas. In order to accomplish this task, they partnered with the Family Health Center, a federally qualified health clinic in McLennan County. The Family Health Center sees 58,000 low-income patients annually (almost 250,000 patient visits a year), and each of their fifteen clinics is located in a food desert.

One of the physicians, Dr. Jackson Griggs, informed me that diet-related disease is the number one preventable disease in the US, over tobacco-related disease. So Dr. Griggs and the farmers of World Hunger Relief decided to do something about it. The farm delivers boxes of locally grown, organically raised vegetables directly to the clinics. The doctors prescribe vegetables to their patients as a treatment for malnutrition and diet-related disease. After their appointments, patients go to the lobby of the clinic, present their prescription, and are handed a box of fresh vegetables. They call the program the Veggie Prescription Program, and thousands of boxes were prescribed to patients in its first year.

Like Dr. Griggs and the farmers of World Hunger Relief, other champions of justice are venturing into the desert to turn five loaves of bread and two fish into thousands of meals for people in need. Regardless of what resources we use to address hunger in our communities, it is our moral imperative to ensure that all people have food to eat.

In 2009, Texas left $6 billion on the table in unused federal and philanthropic dollars allocated to hunger programs that could have greatly reduced hardships for people we have been scapegoating for too long. These underutilized resources may currently exist in your community as well. We left the resources on the table primarily because community leaders were unaware of the existence of the programs or the magnitude of their impact. Whether you choose to pay for food for families from your missions budget at your church, to strengthen utilization of federal resources, or better yet, to create good-paying jobs for people in poverty, that decision is yours and your community's to make. I just want you to know that there are resources at the ready and creative people developing innovative ways to provide food for the hungry.

You are not alone in your desire to put flesh on Christ's command to feed the hungry. Our society may scapegoat the hungry and poor as lazy and undeserving, but there are people providing faithful witness to Jesus's upside-down kingdom all around us. They have foregone power and privilege to commit their lives to the cause of the hungry, and they are adept at identifying resources in the wilderness where most of us see none. Faithful people are providing food for the hungry in every community across America, and they want to walk this path together with you.

—6—

ORGANIZE

How a Shared Response Can Create
Scalable Solutions to Our Communities'
Greatest Social Challenges

Shared Power versus Shaming Power

The godfather of modern-day community organizing is Saul Alinsky, a mid-twentieth-century American Jewish leader who believed the apostle Paul was one of the greatest organizers of all time because of his commitment to establishing the early church.[1] Alinsky's organizing model came with a theory of power. In it, he identified three archetypal models of power: power because of wealth, power because of position in society, and the power of an organized mass of people.[2] Since the poor had neither wealth nor societal status, Alinsky would organize a mass of people to attempt to redistribute power to the poor. His tactic was often successful and necessary to prevent extreme injustices of his era. His tactics have since been used

by politicians and organizers of all types of political persuasions in attempts to amass power, sometimes for the holy cause
of justice and other times for the sheer sake of accumulating
more power.

One of those instances occurred around the late 1990s and
early 2000s. An organized group of residents from a large urban
area actively opposed the construction of a golf course in a
wealthy neighborhood located directly over the city's aquifer.
These concerned citizens were predominantly from low-income
households in one of the city's poorest neighborhoods. The
group was primarily concerned with city funds and tax incentives
being spent on a recreational facility that few in the city would
ever see, let alone use. They were also concerned that building a
golf course over the water supply would contaminate drinking
water for the residents of the community. Their cause was just.[3]

Their process, like many twentieth-century organizing strategies, was to confront the city's "elite" with the sheer quantity
of opposed citizens to publicly shame those proposing the golf
course. So they took to the streets. First, organizers sent mail-
ings to each home in neighborhoods where they had organized
before. Then, organizers invited angry citizens to town hall
meetings where elected officials were invited to show their support for the community's position against the golf course. If
elected officials were in support of building the golf course, the
crowd shouted at them and booed them loudly. If the elected
officials attempted to dance around the issue, choosing not to
address it directly, the crowd booed and jeered. (This tactic is
intimidating. I have attended town hall meetings where this has
occurred. The politicians sweat it out, wondering why they accepted an invitation and looking for a chance to bolt through
the door as soon as the session is over.) Shortly after the series
of town hall meetings, local organizers planned protests at city
hall. When city hall employees and elected officials parked their
cars and walked toward their offices, they were followed by a
crowd shouting at them and holding signs that read, "Kill the
golf course before it kills us!"

Ultimately, the pressure worked. Elected officials voted down the proposal at a city council meeting packed with an organized mass of people opposing the golf course. The group of organized community members had won. However, while it seemed as though the people had garnered power by operating as an organized mass, just as Alinsky had promised decades prior, power was not redistributed in the process. It rarely is. Figuratively speaking, the group of organized citizens won the initial battle but lost the war. The city's elite simply waited a couple of years, garnered more support for their desires, and put together a team of expensive, high-powered lawyers to assist them in their quest to have their golf course. The wealthy community members again took their proposal for a golf course to city hall. This time the proposal passed, and the golf course was built. The influential community members ultimately constructed their golf course because they had considerably more money and more power than the temporary bloc of organized citizens.

The organized group of citizens thought confrontation was the way to justice, as it certainly has to be in many cases. But the confrontational approach has limits and often leads to negative consequences. With this approach, people who are not already on board are rarely converted to the cause of justice. Confrontation, in essence, implies that who is for something and who is against it has already been decided, setting up a self-righteous—and self-defeating—paradigm rarely resulting in compromise, much less in finding common ground. And confrontation almost always ensures powerful enemies to any cause the organizers later take on. For years following the golf course debacle, the city's privileged refused opportunities to assist with the basic needs of the neighborhoods that had opposed their golf course.

Alinsky's concepts of power and the redistribution thereof are just as true today as they were when he began to preach them in the 1940s. But in a time of contention, such as the time we are in now, it seems we need to add a new power to his list, a fourth type of power that can be earned only by cultivating mutual trust: shared power. Ultimately, if we intend to build a system that works for all Americans regardless of their socioeconomic level, we have no choice but to find shared power.

A few years later, the same city set out to reduce homelessness. This time the business community, elected officials, community advocates, and faith leaders all convened to develop a plan—together—to address the growing crisis of homelessness. A public-private coalition to end homelessness was created, strategic plans were developed, and implementation ensued. The result was one of the most progressive, comprehensive approaches to addressing homelessness in the nation. The powerful and the righteous were not pitted against one another but were asked to work together for the benefit of the city's most neglected population. Everyone won with this approach, but only one side wins in a winner-takes-all paradigm.

This city's story of contrasts demonstrates the power of consensus building, of acting based on common ground by engaging a variety of stakeholders. This community brought about social change by developing a centralized infrastructure, redistributing power through shared accountability, and emphasizing community-based ownership. This is how sustainable solutions take shape—by creating shared power rather than shaming power.

Coalitions of the Willing

In 2010, the Texas Hunger Initiative (THI) launched a campaign to end hunger in Texas by 2015. Obviously, we did not accomplish our lofty goal, but the campaign did result in huge gains in the amount of food and resources that became available to food-insecure households. The 2015 goal also became a rallying cry for organizations to work together toward a common goal across for-profit, nonprofit, and governmental sector lines.

After all, hunger affects all communities, so each sector needs to bear its fair share of responsibility.

Ironically, the most difficult task at times is to get nonprofits to work together. People are often surprised to hear that people in the nonprofit sector do not play well in the sandbox with one another. But the reality is that there are not enough resources to meet all the needs in our communities, and nonprofits are inherently set up to compete with one another for charitable resources, government grants, and stakeholders in the community. These people are passionately working to right a wrong and need resources to do so, but with limited resources, their causes, tactics, and organizations are often pitted against one another.

Let me illustrate this point. I had conversations with two prominent nonprofit CEOs when we were establishing the campaign to end hunger in Texas. One told me she believed our idea to address hunger would work, but she and her team would not support it because they did not come up with the strategy and were not the leaders of the campaign. The second put his finger on my chest and chided me about ending hunger. "I don't want you to get credit for making the touchdown when my team and I carried the ball ninety-five yards down the field!" he said.

I explained, "We have over five million food-insecure people in Texas. I think the ball is actually on our own twenty-five, and the federal government gave us the ball at the twenty. So the way I see it, we have seventy-five yards to go, and the only way to take the ball down the field is to do it together. Besides, we are all fine blocking for you and letting you spike the ball in the end zone if we score."

I have been married long enough to know that I may remember events happening one way when everyone else remembers them very differently. It is possible that my self-righteous filter may have misinterpreted the conversations with these CEOs and that their accounts would likely run counter to my own. After all, they had a point. Both organizations had been in the trenches serving food to poor families for decades. Both organizations were also doing so in excellent ways. So having a new guy in town telling everyone that if we all work together we are going to end hunger in five years, when they likely knew better, must have been off-putting. Perhaps if I had asked, "How can I come alongside your goals to end hunger?" the conversations would have gone differently and we would have had an easier time working together instead of butting egos.

Regardless, the problem of hunger is too large and too complex to be addressed by organizations and sectors working independently of one another. And most people and organizations do want to work together and quickly respond favorably to coalition requests. They know that the only way we can comprehensively address hunger is to have an integrated response.

The late sociologist Talcott Parsons wrote that we are living in an era of modern complex systems.[4] He indicated that each sector is performing at the highest levels it ever has. Think about what a neurosurgeon is able to do or how Amazon, Walmart, and UPS have mastered procurement and delivery logistics. The strength of modern complex systems is that we are able to do amazing things like never before in our respective fields. The weakness, however, is that we are so specialized that we speak only the language of people in our own sector, which is limiting. We also have a tendency to overvalue our own sector, thinking all others are lacking something important that makes our role more vital to society. Think about a businessman running for political office touting his business acumen and heralding his lack of experience in politics as a strength. He inherently overvalues the role of the for-profit sector and undervalues our democracy. Or consider academics who act as if earning a PhD made them the most evolved people on the planet and that other people speaking to them can only reduce their brilliance. Or consider do-gooders who self-righteously reflect on the faults of others while failing to look at themselves in the mirror. (Oh, wait—that one hits too close to home.)

Look at what Paul said in his first letter to the Corinthian church:

Now there are varieties of gifts, but the same Spirit; and there are varieties of services, but the same Lord; and there are varieties of activities, but it is the same God who activates all of them in everyone. To each is given the manifestation of the Spirit for the common good. To one is given through the Spirit the utterance of wisdom, and to another the utterance of knowledge according to the same Spirit, to another faith by the same Spirit, to another gifts of healing by the one Spirit, to another the working of miracles, to another prophecy, to another the discernment of spirits, to another various kinds of tongues, to another the interpretation of tongues. All these are activated by one and the same Spirit, who allots to each one individually just as the Spirit chooses.

For just as the body is one and has many members, and all the members of the body, though many, are one body, so it is with Christ. For in the one Spirit we were all baptized into one body—Jews or Greeks, slaves or free—and we were all made to drink of one Spirit.

Indeed, the body does not consist of one member but of many. If the foot would say, "Because I am not a hand, I do not belong to the body," that would not make it any less a part of the body. And if the ear would say, "Because I am not an eye, I do not belong to the body," that would not make it any less a part of the body. If the whole body were an eye, where would the hearing be? If the whole body were hearing, where would the sense of smell be? But as it is, God arranged the members in the body, each one of them, as he chose. If all were a single member, where would the body be? As it is, there are many members, yet one body. The eye cannot say to the hand, "I have no need of you," nor again the head to the feet, "I have no need of you." On the contrary, the members of the body that seem to be weaker are indispensable, and those members of the body that we think less honorable we clothe with greater honor, and our less respectable members are treated with greater respect; whereas our more respectable members do not need this. But God has so arranged the body, giving the greater honor to the inferior member, that there may be no dissension within the body, but the members may have the same care for one another. If one member suffers, all suffer together with it; if one member is honored, all rejoice together with it. (1 Cor. 12:4–26)

The apostle Paul and Dr. Parsons are right. Parsons noted that the only way to be a thriving system in a modern complex environment is to recognize our interdependence.[5] And Paul writes, "For just as the body is one and has many members, and all the members of the body, though many, are one body, so it is with Christ" (1 Cor. 12:12). Doctors can be successful only when they have the right tools; business is largely dependent on infrastructure created by the government; and none of us can live without the honorable role of the farmer. We need one another. We need to learn from one another. We need to be willing to sit together, communicate with one another, and be grateful that we do not have to excel at everything, because our brothers and sisters are in this with us. This is our only chance of tackling our world's greatest social problems.

Dallas Coalition for Hunger Solutions

When we launched our campaign to end hunger in Texas by 2015, we were met with a lot of love in Dallas. Much like in San Angelo, people and organizations in Dallas were ready to work together. It was almost as if they had been waiting for years for someone to give them an excuse. Our town hall meetings were met with tears of compassion for the hungry and excitement for a chance to do something about it with new friends from sectors that had not previously worked together—government and faith communities, nonprofits and businesses all coming together for the common cause of ending hunger in their community. But not everyone immediately stepped up to the plate. There were a few important organizations that seemed to be boycotting the process, one because it believed it was equipped to address the problem of hunger by itself and a few others who found coalition building ineffective—too many meetings, too little action. These arguments are legitimate. We have probably all served on a committee that was futile, such as teams charged with coming up with a "plan" for strategic planning. And some organizations are the LeBron James of community-based nonprofits and could probably come close to winning a game in the playoffs by themselves. But intrinsically, we all know that hunger and poverty are too large for us to tackle by ourselves. We need one another.

Everyone answers to someone, so one key to getting organizations to play well in the sandbox together is by identifying the top dog. In Dallas, it was a member of Congress, and she bought into the idea of a unified shared-power approach to addressing hunger in her community. She became the chair of our coalition efforts and hosted steering committee meetings for the coalition at her office. She expected organizations to attend, and they did. The results were astounding. Over time the organizations that were previously territorial realized they enjoyed working with others. Faith communities stepped up and moved beyond food pantries to engage parishioners to serve the poor. A child hunger action team increased coordination among summer and after-school meal programs and recruited area school districts to serve children three meals a day in high-poverty neighborhoods. A team focused on senior hunger increased access to healthy food and nutrition education to improve healthy aging. And because of the urban agriculture team, urban gardens popped up everywhere. Due to the popularization of collective impact, this coalition model is being widely used across the country to address a wide array of community issues.

By working together, organizations in Dallas transformed a mind-set of scarcity into one of abundance, and it bore literal fruit for the poor.

Hunger Free Community Coalitions

Hunger Free Community Coalitions are critical to cultivating trust and finding common ground in communities, which can lead to transformative change. The language for Hunger Free Community Coalitions was developed and popularized by the Alliance to End Hunger in Washington, DC. The alliance currently supports a network of Hunger Free Community Coalitions across the country and has been a valuable partner to us for the past decade. At THI, we have created a toolkit to support communities adopting such a model. We ourselves support twenty coalitions representing over 60 percent of the population in Texas and have trained communities across the country to implement a model of engagement.

So how do we create and sustain a coalition to end hunger and address the larger problem of poverty in our communities?

On the next several pages, I've provided steps and tactics that are adapted from the Texas Hunger Initiative's "Toolkit for Developing and Strengthening Hunger Free Communities."[6]

Step 1: Recruit Participants

Recently, I visited Burnet, Texas, home to a Texas hill country favorite, Storm's Burgers and Shakes. I met with a hunger coalition that has been active for the past several years addressing needs throughout their rural county. The coalition began with volunteers from one church who saw the need for collaborative action to address hunger. Volunteers initially identified twenty-four entities to approach and with whom to set up one-on-one meetings to learn about the organizations and their leaders, interests, and goals. Most of all, they wanted to build relationships. The result of this outreach was dramatic. Every person they met with came to the first meeting of the coalition. Those attendees also helped to spread the word to other interested organizations and businesses. Seventy-five organizations have since become invested and have contributed in various ways to support the coalition in a rural community. The result was the establishment of the Burnet County Hunger Alliance, which is an active coalition of food pantries, churches, school administrators, elected officials, businesses, and other area leaders who have committed to end hunger in Burnet County, Texas.

Here are a few tactics our team has identified as best practices for recruitment:

- *Conduct one-on-one outreach.* Meet with as many people as possible in a one-on-one setting in order to build relationships and identify what might interest them in getting involved in the coalition.
- *Start with existing relationships.* Reach out first to stakeholders you already know.
- *Consider how you can engage and involve people who have personally experienced food insecurity.* Incorporating community members affected by food insecurity will give you a built-in reality check, add credibility to your effort, and make clear your commitment to a participatory process. Ideally, look for existing grassroots leaders who bring to the table both personal experience and strong relationships with community members. If you neglect this step, you will build a boat that cannot float!
- *Talk to influential people or people with large networks.* Even though they may not become active coalition members, prioritizing outreach to elected officials, faith leaders, and/or civic leaders who can support your effort within the community and introduce you to potential stakeholders is often worthwhile. Of course, you might also gain the benefit of a prominent community leader who wants to play an integral role in the coalition.
- *Make sure the people you recruit to join the coalition reflect the racial, ethnic, and geographic diversity of*

your community, including those you intend to serve.
This will strengthen the coalition's voice and ensure
that you have the experience and perspectives needed to
understand the challenges and opportunities for making
an impact.

- *Use the snowball effect when recruiting.* Get names
from stakeholders and then ask them to help you con-
nect with the people they suggest.

- *Advertise in various ways.* While relationships are at
the core of building a coalition, it is also helpful to
get the word out widely in order to reach those whose
interest you are unaware of or do not have time to engage directly. Some successful ways to get the word out
include social media, community newsletters, organizational newsletters, announcements at other coalition/
association/religious meetings, targeted emails, and
word of mouth.

- *Call to action.* In addition to doing one-on-one outreach to stakeholders, holding one or more group
meetings can be helpful in building energy and excitement for a coalition even before the coalition has been
officially established. A hunger summit is a great way
to bring stakeholders and the general public together to
learn from one another and from experts about food-
insecurity challenges and the initiatives already taking
place in the community to address these issues.

Step 2: Establish a Coalition Structure

South Plains Hunger Solutions organized their coalition
structure with a steering committee that meets quarterly and
three action teams—child hunger, senior hunger, and hunger
and horticulture—that meet monthly. Each action team has a
chair or cochairs who serve on the steering committee, serving
as a connector between the action team and the steering committee. The coalition hosts an annual hunger summit, organized

by the steering committee, at which the action teams update the community on priority projects they have identified, the strategies being used to address them, and subsequent progress.

Ideally, a coalition should have a staff person from a member organization who is committed to serving as the backbone for the coalition. This staff person serves as the coalition coordinator, performing some of the core logistical and administrative tasks needed to maintain an active coalition and support the involvement of community leaders. These tasks include but are not limited to scheduling meetings, securing meeting locations, taking meeting minutes and notes, sending out meeting follow-ups, and maintaining contact lists.

Step 3: Plan for Action

Community assessments are a crucial part of organizing communities for change because they help develop a deeper understanding of a community's strengths, needs, culture, relationships, history, assets, social structure, and conflicts. THI believes in an asset-based approach to community assessment that emphasizes the strengths and resources of a community and utilizes those to develop creative solutions to meet local hunger needs. Working as a coalition to assess your community will help you more effectively take action together.

An asset-based approach to community assessment (often referred to as asset mapping) involves talking to community members—leaders, organizations, and residents—to understand the existing resources, capacities, gifts, and skills that either are already being used or could be used to tackle food insecurity. It often also involves utilizing existing sources of data regarding community assets, such as government data. The most effective and impactful approaches to community assessment engage as many people as possible in the process.

Simply put, you want to identify what each organization is doing, where they are doing it, and what gaps of services exist in the community. The coalition then documents their findings in a report. The report will likely highlight more areas of concern than the coalition should immediately address. Once the report is finalized and shared, the coalition can determine priority areas, develop action teams focused on each priority area, and write a strategic plan outlining the steps the coalition will take to achieve its goals.

Step 4: Take Action

Early in 2009, the CEO of one of Indianapolis's leading nonprofits realized that the impact of the recession was going to create a tsunami of people newly in need and contacted the mayor's office to create a plan. They immediately began to call together interested parties, which led to the creation of the Indy Hunger Network. The emphasis for the initial year was getting to know one another, investigating how things were working, and achieving quick wins to build trust.

Their initial assessment determined that summer hunger was a major problem among children in their community. Local and national figures indicated that only one out of six children in Indianapolis receiving free or reduced-price meals during the school year were receiving food during the summer. The network took action, identifying 150 churches, charities, and schools to participate in a meal program and creating common branding to market summer meals for children. The network recruited a leading marketing firm to develop effective branding. The network's collaborative action resulted in 25 percent more meals being served to children in the summer of 2010.[7]

As you look to implement action plans through work groups, action teams, or task forces, think about some of the following elements to maximize your chances of success:

- *Leadership*. Clearly define who is responsible for guiding the work of each action item, including engaging others in collaboratively implementing the project. This might be your work group, action team, or task force chair or cochairs. Be clear that you are not looking for one person to do a project all alone but to lead a team, even if it is a small team.

- *Logistical support.* What types of logistical support will you need to implement activities successfully? Who can provide that type of support?

- *Training.* Is training needed for coalition members and volunteers to know how to implement the initiative (e.g., community organizing training for coalition members interested in building a community garden)?

- *Target dates.* What are your target dates for accomplishing each activity? Deciding on approximate dates for the completion of each activity creates urgency and accountability.

- *Participants.* In addition to the person playing the leadership role for an activity, who else will participate? Who currently involved in the coalition might be interested in joining? Are there new people you can recruit because they care about the action team's focus area? The more people you can recruit to participate, the more energy there will be to ensure successful implementation.

- *Collaborative decision making.* Engage all members of the action team in learning, sharing, and making decisions together. This is key to ensuring that you are drawing on the expertise and creativity of the entire group and developing the buy-in needed for people to continue to contribute their time and resources.

- *Distribution of tasks.* Make sure that as many team members as possible are given a role to play or a task to implement, even if small. Coalition members will gain more ownership and feel more invested if they are part of doing the work.

- *Resources.* What resources are needed for each activity? Do you need funding or in-kind support for an activity?

If so, who could potentially provide it? Ask the organizations involved in the coalition what they are able to contribute.

- *Location*. Depending on the activity, you might need to identify a location where the activity will take place.
- *Tracking*. How will you track the impact or results of an activity? How will you gather the data you need? How will you plan to compile and share the data with the broader coalition?

Step 5: Assess Progress

The Dallas coalition came out of the gate with a lot of energy, thanks to the congresswoman and a city full of enthusiastic people. The coalition had some initial success, mostly as the result of the work of one of the action teams, but eventually was declining overall in participation and energy. In the spring of 2014, the coalition leadership team conducted a self-evaluation and assessment process to figure out what was working and what needed to be improved. The result was a realignment that led to the creation of five reconfigured action teams focused on specific areas with concrete action plans: child hunger, senior hunger, faith community engagement, urban agriculture, and neighborhood organizing. This new plan reenergized the coalition, engaged new leaders and participants in the coalition, and led to successes in each area.

By assessing your work, your coalition can also identify which tactics were the most successful and which tactics should be altered or changed for the following year. No tactic is perfect; it can always be improved.

When the Hunger Free Community Coalition strategy is paired with the resources outlined in chapter 5, it can become a powerful tool for social change. The model can also be easily adapted to address the larger issues of poverty, human trafficking, homelessness, or other pertinent issues in a local, state, national, or global context. When we paired our Hunger Free

Community Coalition model with child hunger in Texas, we were able to increase meals for children by one hundred million each year since 2011. This could not have happened with just our small team working by itself. This happened because thousands of people and many organizations came together to create public and private partnerships to develop and implement strategic plans for food justice in their communities.

Rosa Parks

Social change is often written and talked about in retrospect, like poetry. It is seen as a spontaneous eruption of passion sprung forth on the world that power structures simply couldn't contain. Our idea of social change is similar to the big bang theory of the universe's origins. A few random and unplanned actions occurred that set off a historical chain reaction.

The story of Rosa Parks is a perfect example of revisionist history. It is widely taught in history classes that Rosa Parks was a tired woman who had worked all day and had to walk a long way to the bus stop. When the bus arrived, there was only one seat available, but it was in a "Whites Only" section. Rosa, tired from a hard day's labor, sat down exhausted in the available seat. This naturally caused outrage on the bus, and the bus driver refused to leave the bus stop until she got out of the seat. She refused and was thrown off the bus. Shortly thereafter, Martin Luther King Jr. swooped in to save the day with a few marvelous speeches (one in front of the Lincoln Memorial), and civil rights legislation was passed. What we rarely hear is that Rosa Parks was in leadership in the Montgomery chapter of the NAACP, and she was not sitting in the "Whites Only" section of the bus but refused to give up her seat to a white man, and that a bus boycott due to someone being thrown off a bus and ultimately arrested had long been discussed.[8] A deeper reading of history and social science tends to discount the myth of unplanned, random action leading to significant social change. Instead, this action was strategically planned and thoughtfully carried out, and a careful dissemination strategy ensued afterward.[9]

Likewise, creating hunger-free communities will take the same level of intentionality, strategy, and careful implementation. Hunger and poverty did not happen overnight, so we will not end them overnight—or with a five-year campaign. But they can be overcome when we recognize that we all have gifts to share and that none of us can tackle hunger alone. We can win only by working together, cultivating mutual trust, finding common ground, and committing our lives to the cause.

7

THE WEST SIDE

Once You Engage a Community, Fear Cannot Hold Out against Love

The Break-in

One evening in 2008, my phone rang repeatedly in the middle of the night. I was startled awake and made my way across the bedroom in the dark to see who was calling with such urgency. I answered the phone, barely awake. It was the police. "Are you Jeremy Everett?"

"Yes. Is everything all right?"

"No sir, your coffee shop was broken into by a gang in the community. They kicked in the glass door and stole your computers. We aren't sure what else is missing. We need you to come down to the shop and look around."

"Okay. I will be right there."

Immediately, Amy asked me what was going on. "Someone broke into the coffee shop. The police are there and want me to come down," I told her.

"Is it safe? Did they catch who did it?"

"I'm not sure. They said it was a local gang. I'll call you when I know more."

I put on my clothes from the previous evening and made the short drive from my house to the shop. When I arrived, there were six police cars out front and a police helicopter flying overhead. The police had already apprehended two of the gang members and recovered a few of the stolen computers. The officers greeted me and began showing me around. The coffee shop was on the corner of a row of buildings in an old neighborhood in San Antonio. It sat right in front of the first public housing unit established in San Antonio, the Alazan Apache Courts. The front door had been kicked in, and glass was everywhere. The flashing lights of the police cars caused the murals inside the shop—murals depicting the story of the West Side that had been painted by Native American youth from the neighborhood—to come alive. It was as if the artists intended them to be seen in the flashing glow of police lights, an occurrence too frequent in the community.

I walked around the shop, trying not to step on broken glass. I could see where the computers had been yanked from the walls and tables and chairs had been knocked over, and I could see a failed attempt to get into our cash register. Fortunately, we had recently upgraded our register at the recommendation of another coffee shop in town. The new register was much heavier than our previous one, which likely made it too difficult to take during this smash-and-grab job.

I was still groggy and in a bit of a fog, as if I were in the middle of a dream. I stumbled back outside to see a couple of the gang members in the back of a police car. My temper flared. I ran over to them and began yelling.

"You could use those computers anytime you want! You didn't steal from me. You stole from the community!"

At the time, only 3 percent of the community had access to a personal computer. Smartphones were not as prevalent as they are now, so our coffee shop was one of the few places in the neighborhood to get free access to computers and the internet.

The gang members did not care. They stared right into my eyes as I yelled at them, attempting to intimidate me. It must have worked at least a little bit because I can still remember the incident well.

After my tense moment with the gang members, I walked back over to talk to the police. They had just been called with a tip about where the gang members had stashed the other computers. Several police cars drove over to the apartment complex to retrieve the stolen items, and sure enough, they were all there. Neighbors of the gang members' stash house had heard the alarm go off at the coffee shop and had watched the gang members run up to their stash house with the shop's computers and a few other things. The neighbors were upset because they knew the shop was *their* shop. The computers the gang stole were the computers they depended on anytime they needed access to technology. They put their own personal safety at risk by calling the cops and snitching on the gang members.

Shortly thereafter, the police returned with the stolen merchandise and helped me unload it and carry it back into the shop. A couple of teenagers who were regulars at the coffee shop walked up during the commotion and offered to help me reinstall the computers. The police stayed until the computers were set back up.

I asked if the police officers could keep a car in front of the shop until morning since the door was kicked in, but they told me they had to move on to calls in other neighborhoods. They had already gone above and beyond that night—for a small shop and eight computers—and I couldn't ask them for more.

As they drove away and the teenagers went home, I was left scratching my head. The door had been kicked in, and I had no way to repair the glass. I couldn't leave to get anything, and it was too late to call anyone to ask for help. So I swept up the glass and pulled up a chair in the doorway to wait until morning, when the first shift would arrive. I called Amy and told her what had happened and that I needed to spend the rest of the night at the shop.

I was feeling a little frightened but mainly vulnerable. It was the middle of the night, and the police hadn't arrested the entire gang. What would stop them from coming back?

Within moments, I saw a crew of people headed my way down the dark street. I was scared to death. As they drew closer, I realized they weren't gang members but several of our regulars at the shop. They lived in the nearby housing projects and had heard all the commotion. They were coming to check on me and their coffee shop community center. I was relieved to see them. A few of the men went home to retrieve tools to help me repair the door. Others helped me tidy up the place so the shop would look nice for the early morning customers.

I don't know how to communicate how big of a deal it was that families nearby reported the break-in. People do not call the police on gangs that live near them. It is a very dangerous proposition. Retaliation is real, and the threat of it can be immobilizing. But our neighbors loved their coffee shop. It was more than a place for them to get coffee. It was one of the best shops in town in a neighborhood that rarely, if ever, got the best. They built it, ran it, and visited it daily. It was respite from the hard life of the housing projects. It was sacred space, and they were not going to let this group of young men destroy it.

We repaired the door with a sheet of plywood, thanks to the men who brought tools and lumber from home, and cleaned up inside. You could hardly tell anything had happened. I was even able to go home and get a few hours of sleep before we needed to open the shop.

The next morning I quickly got a repairman to replace the glass in the front door. Customers came and went, most of whom never knew anything had happened the previous night. But the staff and I sat and talked about what had happened.

While we were talking, the head of the gang walked into the shop with his girlfriend. Without saying a word, he looked around the shop and saw that all the computers had been re-turned, the door had been repaired, and the shop looked great. He obviously was not pleased.

Staying true to my foolish form, I spoke up. "Hey, man, can I help you?" He ignored me and kept staring at the computers. So I spoke louder. "Hey, man, can I help you?" He continued to ignore me and turned to walk out of the shop with his girlfriend quietly, almost stoically, walking behind him.

I should have been relieved at their departure, but I followed them. (I know, I am an idiot.) I followed them right out the door and down the sidewalk, and I said in a very loud voice, "Hey, man, can I help you?"

Everyone walking on the sidewalk stopped in their tracks and began to slowly back away as if they had just seen a mountain lion. They probably had, and I had just provoked it.

This time I got his attention. He turned toward me, slowly took off his jacket, and handed it to his pregnant girlfriend. He was getting ready for a fight. As he squared up, I took a step toward him but put my hands in my pockets, so as to be in a less threatening position. I asked him again, but this time softly, "Can I help you?"

Shaking his head, he said, "Nah, man." He grabbed his coat and walked away with his girlfriend following close behind. She gave me one more glance over her shoulder as they made their way down the street, as if she couldn't believe I was still alive. Honestly, I couldn't either.

I went back into the shop, and the staff stared at me bug-eyed with their mouths gaping open. Finally, Martin said, "Guero, what were you thinking?" *Guero* is slang for "you stupid white man." Martin used it appropriately in that con-text. But the truth is, I was fully aware of what I was doing. I wanted the gang leader to know that his attempts at intimi-dation were not going to be met with cowardice. Nope, they would be met with sheer stupidity—but a well-intentioned stupidity rooted in love and care for a group of people who had shown me the same.

The West Side Community

The coffee shop break-in and resulting community support felt like a high point after much hard work and relationship building. The West Side of San Antonio is an old neighborhood, very old. For over a thousand years, the Native American tribal community there has lived along the Alazan Apache Creek, which runs through the neighborhood. They predate Tejas, Mexico; the independent country of Texas; and Texas as a member of the Union. They have an organization in the neighborhood, American Indians of Texas-Spanish Colonial Missions, dedicated to preserving their history and culture. The organization's offices were across the street from the coffee shop, and its members became some of my teachers during my time in the community. They helped me see that the community was very impoverished but also very strong and tight-knit.

This community was the most empowered community I have ever encountered. This includes rich and poor communities I have lived in or visited around the country. As a Baptist, Anglo outsider in a predominantly Catholic, Hispanic community, my presence could have provoked hostility. After all, for generations there had been white people bearing witness to Christ who had done horrible things to similar communities, including forcing people into slavery and subjugation, bringing disease (sometimes intentionally), and taking land in exchange for "saving souls." This community knew their history, but the residents greeted me with hospitality rather than hatred.

They also communicated clearly to me that I was to listen first. They would introduce me to the community so I could better understand all of the great things happening there and spend time with the organizers, ministers, and activists who had been in the community long before I arrived and who would continue to be committed to the community after I left. The passion, commitment, and professionalism of the community leaders were intimidating. Community meetings were always bilingual, flowing from English to Spanish with the expectation that you could speak both languages. No translation was done or expected. My Spanish was not as strong as it needed to be, but they still expected me to keep up.

I grew up as a kid without a hometown, and the West Side community took me in as if I had been there my whole life. And they continued to force me to face my biases and preconceived notions that I hardly knew were still there.

I confronted one of my biases in the front yard of our West Side home. My wife and I bought a home in the neighborhood shortly after moving to San Antonio. Our neighbors had three generations and close to fifteen people living in a small two-bedroom home with only one window air-conditioning unit in one of the bedrooms. The matriarch and patriarch of the family slept in that room, along with the babies, so they would keep cool on hot south Texas summer nights. In comparison, our house had three bedrooms with central heat and air. Just Amy; our infant son, Lucas; and I lived in our house. We often felt guilty because we had so much more room than our neighbors. We knew that the children and adults living around us were sleeping on the floor or maybe on a couch, spread out all over their homes.

One afternoon I pulled into the driveway after finishing work for the day. I was greeted by Laura, the matriarch of the family next door. She was pruning the rose bush that stood in between our two properties. We made small talk for a while, then she said, "Our family feels so sorry for you."

I asked, "Why is that?"

She said, "Because it must be so lonely living in that big ole house all by yourselves." I laughed and agreed.

When I went inside and told Amy of her comment, we laughed together at the irony of our middle-class framework.

The Mission Center

We moved to San Antonio at the behest of a friend pastoring a large Baptist church in town, and I called him to inquire about job opportunities because Amy was graduating from her master's program and we needed gainful employment. I asked him if he knew of any Christian social action jobs. In his deep, booming voice with a Kentucky drawl, he responded, "Jeremy, I think our church needs to be doing more work on the issue of justice. How would you feel about working for a big ole Baptist church in San Antonio?" Admittedly, I was caught off guard. Amy and I thought our time as Baptists had come to an end. Our values of simplicity and justice did not seem congruent with the Baptist church of the twenty-first century. I think he could sense my hesitation, so he chimed in, "Why don't you come down here and meet me for a beer and we can discuss it?" Now I was really confused. A Baptist preacher had just invited me to discuss an opportunity to work with his church for justice, and we were going to discuss it over a beer!

I gratefully accepted his offer and went to San Antonio to discuss the opportunity. Ultimately, my pastor friend pulled together several organizations for this endeavor—a large Baptist nonprofit as well as local, state, and national Baptist organizations. It quickly became clear that not only were we not done with Baptists but also that I would be working for five Baptist organizations. The unexpected twist was that they were all articulating a desire for justice for the poor. The church provided a rarely used mission center in the West Side to house the ministry.

My first step was to clean out the mission center. I guess because it was a mission center everyone thought it would be the place to donate old clothes (including used underwear and socks) and broken furniture. Ultimately, I took nearly twenty truckloads of garbage to the dump and usable items to Goodwill.

I spent the first year networking with the community. I learned the history and culture of the community. I visited hundreds of organizations to see all the great things being done in the West Side. My hope was to identify gaps of service articulated by the community where we might be able to fill a need. Repeatedly, I heard about the need for an immigrant hospitality house. The West Side was often a first stop for immigrants from Mexico and Central America. They needed a safe place to go and people to assist them in their transition to a new country.

I decided to pull together representatives of the organizations that had hired me and community members articulating the vision. We ate, listened to horrific stories of immigrants making their way to the US, and wept together. As a group, we decided to move forward with the immigrant hospitality house inside the old mission center.

Things started falling into place. We had a little bit of money, enough for us to hire someone to manage the house. We drew up the paperwork, interviewed candidates, and were about to make an offer when my supervisor got a phone call. One of the partner organizations was pulling their support for the project. They said a hospitality house for undocumented immigrants was too controversial for their constituency to support. As a result, we could not move forward with the plan.

I was outraged. We had just spent a year in the community working to earn people's trust. The partners had spent so many evenings meeting and eating with immigrants and community members discussing this very project. How could they bail now?

I drove to their offices and stormed in, incensed. I was full of self-righteous indignation. I demanded to know how they could turn their backs on the people we had gotten to know. That evening and many days following, I fumed and paced the floors of my house. I had known it all along. Baptists were not interested in justice for the poor. Institutions could not be moved toward selfless compassion. They were too busy maintaining the status quo. I wanted to quit in protest, but there was a complicating factor. I could not walk away. I was providing for a family now. We needed the health insurance and salary from my job to live. But I was so embarrassed—humiliated—to return to the West Side and tell the people the news. I assumed they would not work with me anymore. My trust would be broken. I was ashamed.

But they did not respond the way I thought they would. A minister and leadership development coordinator from the community, Don Arispe, listened to my heartbreak. He basically told me to get over myself while also letting me voice my feelings. I am amazed at people who are adept in that way. He reminded me that this was not about me; it was about the immigrants, and in nonprofit work, an initial failed attempt with a community project was the norm. He encouraged me to apologize to community members invested in the hospitality house and to own the failed attempt. After all, I was the broker of the opportunity. I had stirred the waters, so the issue was mine to clean up.

Then Don asked me what I appreciated about the Baptists who had committed to working with me in the first place. He said, "Didn't they give you a job? Don't you have health insurance for your family? They seem to really care about you and your well-being. Do they deserve your judgment?"

He was right. Many of them reminded me of the people I had grown up with as a preacher's kid, people who had always showed hospitality and compassion to my family when we arrived in a new town not knowing anyone. Like those people who had raised me, these folks cared for me and my family too. But I was so angry with them. We had broken bread with people, wept with them, and now we were turning our backs on them.

Don asked me, "Why do you think they were willing to work with you from the beginning?"

"I don't know," I said.

He said, "It's probably because they care about justice too. Perhaps you just asked them to take on too much out of the gate."

I asked, "What do you mean, Don?"

"You grew up like these folks, right? You were raised with similar values and concerns . . . a similar worldview, right?"

"Yes," I said, "but I don't see the world like that anymore. After my experience encountering the story of St. Francis . . ."

"I know, Jeremy. I have heard your story," Don said. "You know I am grateful for what God is doing in your life. But God is working in their lives too. To be a good organizer, you have to listen first. I know you have spent the year listening to people from the neighborhood, but have you listened to the people who brought you here in the first place? Your job is to really listen. Listen to us. Listen to them. Understand what is happening in our culture. Reflect on that theologically. Then you will know how and when to move forward."

When we moved to the West Side, Amy told me to simply see where God was moving and then join in. I thought we had been called to the West Side to be brokers of justice for the poor. I did not realize that the poor would teach me how to broker justice with the wealthy.

Guadalupe Street Coffee

I took Don's advice and went through my notes from the first year and circled back with community leaders, who were quick to forgive my failed attempt at establishing a hospitality center, and our Baptist partners, who forgave my self-righteous outrage. What I heard repeatedly was that we needed to strengthen educational opportunities and outcomes for our high school students. I also heard there was a need for economic development and employment opportunities in the community. One other item that was mentioned time and again was that, in an age of Starbucks on every street corner in many parts of the city, our neighborhood of more than 150,000 people did not have a coffee shop. Maybe a coffee shop would be a good place to start.

The community *and* the Baptists loved this idea. The community developers loved the idea because they could use it to leverage businesses to relocate their offices to our neighborhood, which was only a stone's throw away from downtown but offered rental space at half the cost. The Baptists loved it because they believed strongly in employment opportunities and education, and a coffee shop would employ residents and provide after-school tutoring for the high school students in the community. The activists' liked it because we could take down the "Mission Center" sign and replace it with a new business sign, a sign of opportunity, a sign of empowerment.

Speaking of signs, the activists had asked me early on, "How many mission centers do you see in wealthier communities?"

I thought for a second. "None," I said.

They responded, "That's right, because people assume rich people can do things for themselves but that the poor need the rich to help us with basic functions. We work hard. We have ambitions for a better life. What we need are good-paying jobs, not someone's old underwear." The mission center's presence reinforced the false notion that this community was less than. This certainly wasn't the intent of the congregation who had founded it, but it was the reality to the community.

I reconvened community stakeholders, the Baptist organizations, and a few potential funders to begin planning for the establishment of Guadalupe Street Coffee—the West Side's first coffee shop and San Antonio's first social enterprise. The community was abuzz with excitement. The young and the old helped with demo day. The tribal community offered artists to paint murals on the inside walls to match the beautiful murals outside other important community buildings. A member of my small congregation who was a contractor offered to build the shop's coffee bar and hand make tables. The signs and logos were designed, and in a few months the coffee shop was born—just in time for a soft opening on Día de los Muertos.

The goal of Guadalupe Street Coffee was to be the nicest coffee shop in San Antonio. To make that a reality, Katarina Velasquez, the owner of a coffee shop on the Riverwalk (who also happened to be the daughter of the legendary community rights activist Willie Velasquez), volunteered her time to set up our coffee supplier, order us the best espresso machine in the business, and train the staff. She even took weeks off from her own shop to help us run ours. Her father had died tragically when she was very young, but before he died, he started the Southwest Voter Registration and Education Project in the 1970s to register the Latino and Hispanic communities so they could not only vote but also run for office. The organization's original office was right next door to Guadalupe Street Coffee. Life was coming full circle for Katarina. We could not have opened the shop without her or any of the other community stakeholders, Baptists included.

The grand opening was a special event. Hundreds packed into the shop, shoulder to shoulder, laughing, telling stories, trying coffee and treats. Then City Councilwoman Patti Radle made her way to the stage. The community called her La Rosa, and she was known for her passion and the love she had for the West Side. As the story goes, she didn't actually run for city council, but the community took to the streets and ran a campaign for her. To both her surprise and maybe chagrin, she won overwhelmingly. Her speech at the grand opening was fiery, as if she were possessed by the spirit of the prophet Isaiah. She pumped her fist in the air and shouted, "We deserve a nice coffee shop!" Members of the crowd pumped their fists and replied, "Que viva!" Then she said it again, as if we did not hear her the first time. "We deserve a nice coffee shop!" Then the crowd repeated, "Que viva!"

I sat to the side in sheer amazement while holding our oldest son, Lucas, watching this crowd singsong back and forth with the councilwoman. Amy stood next to me holding our newest addition, Samuel. She could tell I was tearful, and I could feel her looking at me with eyes of gratitude. She knew that a year prior to this day I was ready to walk away. She was proud of me for sticking it out. I turned and saw Don in the room. He cheered with the rest of the crowd, then glanced over at me with a look that said, "I told you so."

The shop was a success by many standards. We were packed full with people from all walks of life—politicians, executives, ministers, abuelas and abuelos, and teenagers. The computers had a daily waiting list. We had more applicants for barista jobs than we could have imagined. Our manager, Lourdes, was asked to run for city council when Patti's term ended. Everything went well, but we did not sell as much coffee as we had hoped. My boss would laugh and tell me, "Jeremy, you run a great program but a bad business. Maybe there was a reason Starbucks didn't open up a shop on the West Side." He was certainly right, but the coffee shop was the center of the community. It became our hospitality house, just in a way I did not initially imagine.

Shortly after the shop opened, I was approached by a group of stakeholders that was very interested in learning about our plans for a hospitality house for immigrants. I told them of our initial plans, and after a period of discernment and prayer, they opened a hospitality house for the undocumented.

Saint Maria of College Prep Programming

We wanted the coffee shop to be a place for after-school tutoring. It turned out that our idea to recruit local college kids to hang out at the shop to be available to the high school students and assist them with homework was not viable. Not because the college students were unwilling or the high school students did not come to the shop. When school let out, we were often overrun with students. The problem was that our schools were so poorly funded that they had only a class set of textbooks, which meant no homework for the students. Many of us were horrified to learn the news. This meant that even our valedictorians were graduating unprepared for the rigors of university life. On a similar note, during my five years in the neighborhood, no college recruiters visited the high schools, but the US military was there on a weekly basis. If you are wondering what inequality looks like, then look no further. We honestly did not know what to do to support our students, even though strengthening educational opportunities was supposed to be one of our core functions.

Well, ask and ye shall receive. One afternoon the coffee shop door blew open with the sound of thunder and a flash of bright light, and there appeared Maria Fernandez. Okay, maybe it was not quite that dramatic of an entrance. It was probably more like a professionally dressed woman holding a large bag and a number of giant three-ring binders while trying to open our squeaky door, eventually getting it open without dropping all of her notebooks, shuffling over to the barista, and asking where she could find me. I was sitting near the coffee bar watching this hilarity unfold. When the barista, Martin, pointed her to my table, she walked over, dropped her enormous binders on it, and fell into a chair across from me. "Hello, I am Maria, and our mutual friend Don sent me to you. I run a college prep program called Vista, and I would like to run it out of your coffee shop. I don't need funding. I have my own. I care about our kids, and I want to see them escape poverty by going to college. An entire family must apply to be a part of my program, because the parents of our kids need to buy into this as much as the students. If the parents and their children focus on the goal of graduating from college, then graduating from high school is a foregone conclusion."

"Maria, you had me at hello."

Maria did exactly what she said she would do. She ran her Vista program out of Guadalupe Street Coffee and ran it to perfection. Students applied as young as eighth grade and as late as junior year of high school. Students and parents were at the coffee shop from after school until closing. They also came on Saturdays and Sunday afternoons. Maria had a 100 percent college placement rate with her students, earning her the nickname St. Maria of College Prep Programming.

With, not *For*: Asset-Based Community Development

Ultimately, we succeeded with most of our goals at the coffee shop. We provided employment to community residents and became a place of hospitality—a community center for all walks of life. The coffee shop was also a place of educational preparation to assist students on their paths toward financial freedom, and we leveraged several businesses to relocate to the community that hired the great folks from the West Side. We were recognized for the work, first by the City of San Antonio, winning the Redevelopment Project of the Year Award, then by the *Austin American Statesmen* as a place you must visit when traveling to San Antonio.

People would often come to spend time with me at the shop to learn how to replicate the coffee shop in their community. I would tell them the shop was not worth replicating. The principles of trust, collaboration, and commitment were what they needed to replicate.

Because I chose to buy a house in the community, to listen and learn about the history and culture of the community, and not to show up with an outsider view of the problem that only I could solve, trust was ultimately established. Once the community trusted me, even when I made blunders, they were willing to continue the work. Our commitment was to the cause of the people—that is worth replicating.

What I learned from my experiences in Christian community development is that the poor are our brothers and sisters. "We are all related," as my Native American friends would remind me. Dr. King put it eloquently: "We are caught in an inescapable network of mutuality, tied in a single garment of destiny. Whatever affects one directly, affects all indirectly."[1] The American antihunger community and faith communities need to hear that message. We are great at using research to inform our programs for the hungry, we are great at addressing the logistical needs of hunger, and we are great at recognizing the need for a strong commitment to public policy and advocacy. But we treat the poor as clients, as problems to be solved. That is not the case. For change to happen for the hungry, they must lead the charge. The West Side showed me how to work *with*, rather than *for*, the people. I am grateful for their tutorial.

The Break-in Story Continued

When I got back inside the coffee shop after confronting the gang leader, my coworkers and I discussed the incident. We all felt threatened. If the leader of the gang was willing to show up in broad daylight in a shop full of patrons to survey the damage his subordinates were supposed to have created, we knew he was not someone to be messed with.

I called my bosses and asked for advice. The gang members hung out right behind the shop. They knew the cars we drove and where many of us lived. I was beginning to second-guess my decision to confront the gang members the night before and certainly that morning. My bosses encouraged us to close the shop for a while and leave town for the weekend, if not longer. So we did. We closed the shop. Staff members went to stay with relatives in other parts of town. We traded cars with a friend who lived across town so no one would recognize the car parked in our driveway just blocks from the shop.

The major difference for me between this incident as opposed to the incident on 15th Street in Waco years earlier was that this time I had a family. Amy and my two children were in my life now. I had more to lose. The fear of retribution was overwhelming.

Love was not winning. Fear was choking love like a seedling among thorns.

After being closed for a few days, I called the staff on Sunday night to see how they were doing. They were okay. So we decided to meet at the coffee shop Monday morning to decide what to do. We didn't open the shop to the public. We just sat around a table and talked about how we were feeling and whether to shut the place down for a while.

We knew that our decision would impact the community. After all, opening the shop was such a communal experience. Community members had even rallied to our support in the middle of the night after the break-in. This shop was not merely about those of us who worked there. It was emblematic of the strength of the West Side community. Instead of closing, we decided to open the shop and throw the neighborhood a party—a party of appreciation for all they meant to us and for all they had done to make the shop a community center.

We borrowed a giant grill and parked it as close as we could to the Alazan Apache Courts, where the gang members congregated, and sent flyers around the community. Guadalupe Street Coffee was having a party, and all were invited. We invited the police officers who had helped us, the community members who had rallied to our cause in the middle of the night, our regulars, and even the gang members.

We were not going to be ruled by fear. If we really believed love was stronger than fear, we would put it to the test.

The community came in droves. We served everyone until we were all full of food and laughter. We reopened the coffee shop and made sure the gang members knew they were always welcome. One of the gang members took us up on our invitation and became one of our regulars. I remember watching him with joy a year later as he worked at a computer he had once tried to steal, sitting next to an abuelita from our neighborhood and making small talk as they sipped their cappuccinos.

The other gang members were not interested in joining us, but the community was no longer tolerant of their intimidation. So the gang moved on, and love won.

8

POLITICS

Searching for Consensus amid
a Landscape of Contention

Reawakened Political Activism

I love politics. I am almost ashamed to admit it. I think my love
for politics initially emerged when we were living in Arkansas
during my elementary and middle-school years. The Speaker
of the Arkansas House, Lacy Landers, was a member of our
congregation. I remember sitting with him in his big chair and
playing with toy cars on his podium, while he presided over the
Arkansas legislature and laws were being discussed. I remember, as I grew older, being a page in that same room for elected
officials, running notes back and forth between members and
their staff, waiting impatiently. My father was the chaplain of
the House during part of our time in Arkansas. He and Gov-
ernor Bill Clinton would routinely make hospital visits or pray

with elected officials. Politics was engaging, entertaining, and fast paced. I loved it.

My love of politics grew throughout high school, where I performed well in mock congress (which was my only accomplishment in high school, other than algebra—I was so good at algebra that my teachers asked me to take it twice!), and on into college, where I took an interest in what was happening on campus and in the community of Birmingham.

My love for politics went dormant, however, after my experience of St. Francis's story and feeling my call to the poor. Prior to that calling, I could imagine myself running for office one day, but after my calling, my interest was intensely focused on immersing myself in the throes of America's poorest communities. It was not until the election of 2008 that my love for politics came back in full force.

The West Side of San Antonio became a battleground neighborhood for the Barack Obama and Hillary Clinton campaigns, both vying for the Hispanic vote. Both campaigns set up offices in San Antonio's West Side, and their workers became regulars at Guadalupe Street Coffee. The coffee shop was ground zero, and I was in political heaven. Daily politicos from across the country would come to the shop to drink coffee, meet with campaign teams, and woo potential voters. One of the highlights of my time on the West Side was debating the merits of Obama against the merits of Clinton with Henry Cisneros, former Housing and Urban Development secretary and mayor of San Antonio; his wife, Sandra, a city councilwoman; Antonio Villaigosa, the mayor of Los Angeles; and Lourdes Galvan, our coffee shop manager and a city council representative. I was considerably outmanned—four against one. They were national politicians with more charm, wit, and tenacity in one finger than I would have in a lifetime. These suited-up politicians likely destroyed this sloppily dressed community activist in our political debates, but it didn't matter. I was having the time of my life.

Obama, a senator at that time, came to our coffee shop when he visited the West Side. He took the time to shake the employees' hands before walking across the street into the El Parian outdoor amphitheater and holding a town hall meeting for hours. The former community organizer had his sleeves rolled up, used a few familiar lines, and spoke from the heart about his hopes for America. I had never witnessed anything like his coming to the West Side. People lined up for blocks to try to see him. Students climbed in trees and on top of buildings to catch a glimpse of him.

You may not agree with his politics, or you may think Obama was a bad president. I certainly critiqued his every move once he was elected. But that experience reawakened the fire of political activism in me that had become dormant from my early years. It helped me realize that politics could be a vehicle for positive change for the hungry and poor in our country and around the globe. But how we go about it can have huge implications, for good or for bad.

P3 and the Syrian Refugee Crisis

A few years after Obama visited San Antonio, I found myself in the middle of political discussions and debates on the state and federal levels. The Texas Hunger Initiative (THI) was asked to partner with the Texas state agency administering poverty programs, such as SNAP (the Supplemental Nutrition Assistance Program, formerly called Food Stamps) and Medicaid, and with advocacy organizations in order to retool service delivery. The state had been in a budget crunch, which forced the agency to close approximately one hundred regional offices a few years prior, reducing access to these federal programs in midsize towns and rural communities where the offices were closed. This action not only created hardship for already struggling families and the employees laid off from the agency but also made the agency noncompliant with federal regulations regarding access. So THI worked with the agency and the advocates to create an online platform and a single, integrated application for all the benefit programs, saving the state a lot of time processing cumbersome paper applications.

We also created a model for a third party to recruit community organizations to offer application assistance. The third party was a consortium of nonprofits—faith leaders, healthcare providers, and antihunger advocates—who spoke the language of their sectors and could recruit and train organizations in their respective networks. Members of this public-private partnership, or P3, acted as emissaries, translating the language and regulations of the state into a language and a process their networks could understand. The P3 consortium ultimately recruited and trained fourteen hundred community-based organizations during a four-year period to become access points for low-income families to apply for federal assistance.

One of the unintended benefits of the model is that these community-based organizations (congregations, nonprofits, food pantries, etc.) now existed in their community with a strong sense of mission and purpose. Those with a Christian faith perspective did their work to put flesh on Jesus's command to feed the hungry, clothe the naked, and provide the homeless with shelter. They wanted to not only help the families with benefits assistance but also minister to the whole family. These social workers, faith leaders, and community volunteers served as guides to families needing additional assistance to get by, similar to the role an investment banker may provide to wealthier clients wanting to figure how and when to retire. The program was a success. The fourteen hundred organizations helped to increase participation in federal programs by more than 15 percent, putting billions of dollars in resources into the pockets of low-income Texans for food and health care. Their work also made financial sense. The state saved hundreds of millions of dollars by using the online application rather than the cumbersome paper application and having community-based organizations be the access points rather than one hundred state offices, each with employees, rental costs, and so forth. This is another example of how shared power—all sectors working together in a public and private partnership—can make a systemic improvement for the hungry in our communities.

Unfortunately, that is not the end of the story. At the same time this new benefits application model was taking shape, articles began to surface highlighting the horrific treatment Syrians were facing at the hands of Bashar al-Assad, and countries around the world were responding with a willingness to provide asylum to refugees. These events seem completely unrelated, but Texas refused to receive any refugees, a decision that created tension between justice advocates and state leaders. Faith communities believed strongly that Texas should provide shelter to those who had suffered horrific tragedy at the hands of an evil regime, but our state leaders disagreed, vehemently warning of Muslim terrorists pretending to be displaced refugees in order to sneak into our state to do us harm. Their concerns were real, but the faith communities' cause was just.

So an organization affiliated with the P3 consortium was moved to action. In an effort to get the attention of state leaders—elected officials, political appointees, and so on—they wrote letters and op-eds demanding we welcome refugees and demonizing the politicians for being unwilling. Their hope was that public shaming would cause the politicians to change their minds or at least their policy. Just like the group fighting the golf course in San Antonio, this group was on the right side of justice, but their tactics proved to be not only unpersuasive but also damaging to the communities they served.

State leaders were outraged by the public shaming and looked into the organization behind it. When they found the organization had a contract with the state and was playing a leadership role in providing the poor with federal benefits access, the state leaders attempted to end the program. When that did not work—because it was legislatively created—they canceled the contract with the P3 consortium and slowly strangled the initiative until it failed to exist.

From my perspective, the faith-based organization's desire for Texas to provide a place of refuge for our brothers and sisters across the globe was right and just. But the tactic of shaming the powerful didn't just fail to change the minds of the powerful, it also motivated them to look for ways to hurt those opposing their interests. Once again, the shared-power approach proved to be life-giving—generating the model to increase access, nutrition, and health—and the shaming-power approach proved to be life-taking. When we are operating on a state or federal level, politics can be catastrophic when we get it wrong.

Demonizing those we are trying to persuade does not work. It does not work in a one-on-one confrontation (imagine a marriage counselor encouraging a couple to shame and humiliate their partner as a way of solving conflict) or as a long-term political tactic to make our world a more just place. Ultimately, we just end up embodying the hate we say we are fighting against.

When we choose a shared-power approach and take time to cultivate common ground with people on opposing sides, we are participating in a nonviolent social change strategy. We are honoring the other by listening to their point of view and doing the hard, laborious work of cultivating trust and finding common ground when it is possible.

Conversely, when we choose to shame or to demonize the other, we are committing an act of violence. When we choose this path, we become comfortable with the ends justifying the means, and we take on characteristics that we may not have liked about the other from the onset. Our hatred of a policy becomes a hatred of the person bringing it forth. We also assume that our side is right and good. Therefore, we possess truth and justice, and the other side represents unjust evil. But aren't all of us full of mixed motives? Certainly. Are any of us perfect? Of course not. Some decisions we make and actions we choose are good and just. Other actions reflect our sinful nature. And none of us are omnipotent. We need one another.

If we think our community, our political party, or our denomination is the sole possessor of truth and thus the world simply needs to do what we tell them, we are fooling ourselves. If we think Democrats can come up with solutions to make the world a better place without Republicans and vice versa, we are fooling ourselves.

A cornerstone of the Christian belief system is that we are created in the image of God. That is our starting point, our point of origin. We need to honor that each of us is created in God's image, whether black or white, Muslim or Christian, man or woman, Republican or Democrat. A winner-takes-all battle always ends up hurting the disenfranchised the most. Because while we become consumed with anger for the other, the poor and hungry are not eating. While we hurl insults at the other, they have no health care. While we speak "truth," they are being evicted from their homes.

This is not to say that collaboration and finding common ground will be without conflict. Conflict is inherent as we work toward peaceful solutions to social injustices. Conflict abounds when we engage in coalition meetings with people who have different models of facilitating meetings, when our personalities conflict with those of our coworkers, or when we disagree on policy solutions. However, we can experience conflict and still honor the createdness of the other. I'll repeat that: you can experience conflict and still honor the createdness of the other. Choosing to take the other side seriously, without dismissing their point of view, is a way to honor their createdness. When we choose to do this, we are moving the world toward justice, toward shalom.

Our tactics and strategies must reflect the integrity we hope to achieve for our cause. If we believe Jesus calls us to a higher ethic of loving our neighbor, then we must work hard to ensure that those we see as barriers to justice are treated with the love and respect that their createdness demands. In so doing, we participate in "bending the universe towards justice"[1] regardless of the outcome of our cause.

This is not to suggest that the confrontational approach should never be utilized. Dealing with gun violence in America, immigrant children being separated from their parents, and politicians lacking the fortitude to do something about these issues may require a confrontational approach. But the confrontational approach is only one method of social change and should be used only as a last resort. And because it is a dangerous method that too often leads to dehumanization of the other side, it should be used with careful intention as we keep our collective createdness in the image of God at the forefront of our minds and our actions.

Our political system has become toxic, with both sides preferring to cast stones at the other side rather than coming together to find common ground for the common good. We want our side to win, which necessitates the other side must lose. Both sides believe they are at war. Casualties happen in war. Unfortunately, as with the hurricane in New Orleans, the casualties are too often the poor.

The Commission

My experience with the National Commission on Hunger highlighted why our current system of power dynamics is so limited in addressing domestic hunger and poverty and why we need to develop a shared power.

Congress appointed ten members to the National Commission on Hunger, five appointed by Democrats and five by Republicans. We spent much of the first year at an impasse while working together in Washington, DC. I think this was in large part because we did not trust the perspectives of the appointees from the other party. If a conservative made a recommendation, the progressives assumed they were just trying to find ways to abandon the federal government's responsibility to care for the hungry. If progressives offered a recommendation, the conservatives assumed they were just trying to grow the welfare state and abdicate personal responsibility. I wish I could say I rose above the rhetoric, but I am hardwired to argue for the sake of arguing. My parents joked that, as a child, I got into a fierce debate with a telephone pole in our front yard. To this day I believe I came away from that debate victorious.

Fortunately for the commission, we elected two coleaders appointed by opposing political parties. The two could not have been further apart politically, but they were both natural leaders and intellectual equals. They also were both committed to the commission making consensus recommendations to Congress and the secretary of the United States Department of Agriculture after the completion of our term. This commitment to consensus kept us moving forward, trying to find ways toward common ground. One of the members encouraged us to break bread together after our meetings. We did, and those dinners led to conversations about our families, our career ambitions, our faith perspectives, and so forth. One of my fellow commission members was about to have his first grandbaby at the same time Amy and I were expecting our third child. Shortly after their births, we giddily exchanged pictures of the newborn babies to the delight of another commission member who was a pediatrician. We talked about topics as varied as football and university politics, and I even received guidance about leading a nonprofit while maintaining a commitment to family.

This bonding may seem trivial, but it is how we began to trust one another. It was over dinner that we realized our collective commitment to the poor and hungry in our nation, which in turn cultivated a commitment to one another. It is often said by political commentators that the breakdown in DC is due to politicians no longer living in Washington. In the past, Republicans and Democrats could disagree about policy during the day but coach their children's little league games together or smoke cigars together in the evening. Spouses of our elected officials would spend time together, run in similar social circles, and attend church together.

Two former congressmen I greatly admire are Frank Wolfe (R-VA) and Tony Hall (D-OH). They are well-known on the Hill as champions for the hungry, and they became friends through a prayer ministry they formed together. Their friendship became so strong that they ultimately bought homes next door to each other after they retired. The reason these types of relationships are critical for our democracy to be strong is because people such as Frank and Tony would never get on the news and demonize each other. They knew that though they had differing political persuasions, they both were rooted in their faith in Christ. So they trusted each other deeply, even when they disagreed. Over time they learned they had more in common than they initially thought. They put aside some of their differences because of their common commitment to the health and well-being of the hungry. Trust, commitment, and collaboration were virtues they manifested in their tenures in Congress.

Recently, things in DC have been a little different. Now all that seems to matter is that one side can claim victory. An article written by Ezra Klein just before one of President Obama's State of the Union addresses summed it up well. Klein likened politics to a football game, with each political party as an opposing team.[2] As the article pointed out, in football we don't pull for our team to tie—we want to win. Likewise, today's politicians are not being encouraged to build consensus or to compromise and come to a mutually beneficial tie. Rather, today's political state of the union is a winner-takes-all battle. In this paradigm, the goal is an accumulation of power, and strengthening our nation is an afterthought.

The commission was committed to consensus, which is likely the most prophetic stand anyone can take in DC during this period in US history. We also knew we needed to get out of the Beltway and back into communities to spend time with the people experiencing hunger and the organizations addressing it. These travels bonded us to a greater degree and continued to move us beyond politics to find ways to reduce hunger through policy.

Testimonies such as Professor Sharkey's and community members and activists sharing their stories and opening their homes to us were incredibly formative. On a visit to a tribal community, we were stunned by the hospitality of a group of impoverished Native Americans who made us a meal and shared their accounts of tribal life. As part of their prayer prior to the meal, they passed an empty plate, and each of us took some of our food and placed it on the plate as a way of honoring their elders who had died and reminding us of those in need among us.

One profound moment came while visiting a community center in a *colonía*. We were escorted into a small room with no air-conditioning in 100-degree desert heat. We were greeted by more than a dozen women who sat in the room awaiting our arrival. They were prepared to share their stories with us about food insecurity and hardship. We could tell this was going to be rough. The women had the lost look of soldiers returning from war. Their eyes were glazed with a deep sadness due to profound loss. They did not want to be there with us, but they mustered up the courage to let us know about their experience.

The women had escaped to the US, fleeing the cartel violence that had erupted in the Mexican city of Juarez, right across the border from El Paso. Many of them had lost loved ones to gang violence, and several mentioned that the cartels had tried to recruit them or their children for work as gang members or prostitutes. These women had been left with few options other than to flee to the US for safety.

Once they arrived, they found work as custodians in hotels, machine factories, and local restaurants. Each woman told her story of working often more than eighty hours weekly, and all their employers had chosen not to pay them at some point. The employers would make excuses for why these women should not be paid. If the women confronted them, the employers would threaten to call immigration.

Unfortunately, their stories continued. They told us that each of them had experienced sexual violence and death threats since arriving in the US, all at the hands of American citizens. One woman said her supervisor repeatedly forced her to have sex with him in his office, knowing that she would not call the police on him for fear of deportation. She had escaped the sexual violence of cartels only to fall prey to sexual violence in the US.

The women knew hunger. They knew profound hardship. They tried to keep tears at bay while telling us their stories, but when the tears penetrated the surface, they came like a flood—for them and for us.

"'Lord, when was it that we saw you hungry and gave you food, or thirsty and gave you something to drink? And when was it that we saw you a stranger and welcomed you, or naked and gave you clothing? And when was it that we saw you sick or in prison and visited you?' And the king will answer them, 'Truly I tell you, just as you did it to one of the least of these who are members of my family, you did it to me'" (Matt. 25:37–40).

There are many morals to this story. First, if you are demonizing the immigrants crossing our border hoping for a better life for their families, I hope these stories give you greater understanding. They are our brothers and sisters. They did not choose where to be born. They do not want to leave their homes for a place where people do not treat them with respect and dignity. They are doing so only out of a sense of desperation. In a perfect world, it would be preferable for these families to apply for asylum in the US and be granted legal, safe passage prior to violent acts committed against them by warring cartels. Unfortunately, cartels don't wait on the US government to process paperwork, so families are often forced to flee prior to receiving any type of documentation.

Second, there are many people out there who have given themselves over to their base nature, that is, their sinful nature. They are in every segment of society. But there are also many people who have given themselves over to the good. These immigrant women met one another at a community center established by other immigrant women for the sole purpose of caring for people experiencing unimaginable hardships. We are all created in God's image. This is hard to see in some people, but in others it radiates throughout their being. We should all strive to be like them.

Stories such as this one—and others from my time hearing from individuals living in poverty on tribal lands, in urban low-income communities, and across the rural Southwest—illustrate the dire problem in our country and demonstrate the need for our legislators and decision-makers to work together to find solutions that will benefit the common good and not just a select group of constituents. Fortunately, the commission was able to make twenty consensus recommendations.[3] Doing so was not easy, as we spent the last two months debating and discussing the merits and potential detriments of our final list of recommendations. But recommendations were made, congressional testimony was given, and the secretary received our bipartisan report.

A Congressman

Early in my tenure at THI, I was introduced to a US congressman whose help we desperately needed. A community we were working in was in crisis. The people were isolated by geography, and poverty was so rampant that when a local food bank would offer food distribution, the line would be over a mile long. People were desperate.

My colleagues and I met with the congressman to ask for his help in addressing the crisis. His response was immediate: "Tell 'em to move. We have jobs in my district. If they really need food, they wouldn't live there. If the town is that poor, it just needs to die."

I sat there stunned. I could not believe he was actually saying these things. When he was done speaking, he stood up and shook our hands, and we were escorted out of his office. Outside in the hallway of the congressional building, my colleagues and I tried to process what had just occurred. By that evening, our shock had turned to anger. I wanted to shame him as publicly as I could. But no reporters knew my name or likely cared about this small town enough to talk to me. So I called my dad for counsel. He encouraged me to build a relationship with this congressman. My dad said, "Well, at least you know where he stands, right?"

"I guess so."

"He is a Christian, right?"

"Yes sir."

"Next time you meet with him, remind him where Jesus stands."

I took his advice and spent time meeting with this congressman over the next ten years, reminding him that we are our brother's keeper and that this means we need to feed the hungry. My goal was to slowly introduce him to the complexities of hunger and poverty to see if I could change his mind.

On one of my trips to Washington, DC, to visit with him, he seemed more eager to talk with me than on my prior trips. I walked into his office, and he almost seemed enthused to greet me. His staff was a little kinder and more hospitable as well. My curiosity was piqued. Why were they acting so . . . weird?

"Jeremy, I was just in my district, and my staff arranged for me to meet with different hunger ministries. I told them we didn't have hunger in our district. We have some of the lowest unemployment rates on the American record! But they said to come and see what these constituents had planned. Jeremy, you would not believe this, but I met with an elderly couple who had been schoolteachers their whole lives. They went to church, raised good kids, and retired on a pension. But they couldn't afford to stay in the home they had owned for decades because of skyrocketing inflation in our area, much less afford a gallon of milk. Jeremy, they had done everything right, but they were hungry! We gotta do something about this."

My dad was right. Over time this congressman came around. He is still no Tony Hall, George McGovern, or Frank Wolfe on the issue of hunger, but he is making strides. I was tempted to throw him under the bus. I likely would have if a reporter had come up to me after that first meeting. But that would have ended any potential for a relationship I could have built with the congressman, which again would have hurt the hungry and poor more than it hurt me. If we are going to change our country for the better, we need to say enough to politics as a winner-takes-all battle and instead come together to give voice to all Americans.

I have seen God at work among impoverished communities in America, in the hearts and minds of elites, and even in the halls of political power. Because of these experiences, I am convinced that the uniting power and prophetic witness of sowing seeds of mutual trust, collaboration, and commitment are critical to cultivating hunger-free communities in our time of contention. My hope is that by bridging the cultural and ideological divide, we can find a more effective way to alleviate suffering and advance justice for the hungry.

History teaches us that how we go about change should reflect the integrity of our desired outcome. When we channel self-righteous indignation and anger and belittle those with whom we disagree, even when they are perpetuating an injustice, we do not win in the end. Dr. King famously said, "Hate cannot drive out hate, only love can do that."[4] We need a new way of addressing hunger and poverty in America. Hate is not driving it out.

9

TOGETHER AT THE TABLE

The Texas Hunger Initiative's Story
of Organizing a Systemic Response to Hunger

In chapter 6, I laid out five steps to create a Hunger Free Community Coalition. This chapter tells the story of our work at the Texas Hunger Initiative (THI) and how it came to be. I refer to the steps I recommended earlier and apply them to our statewide effort. You will notice that these steps are not always linear, and occasionally I have repeated steps toward the goal of getting everyone to work together with the common goal of addressing hunger both locally and statewide.

Step 1: Recruit Participants

My friends Bill Ludwig and Don Arispe could not be more different. Bill is a farmer turned bureaucrat from north Louisiana.

He wears tight jeans, boots, and a sport coat, and the top two buttons of his dress shirt have not met each other in the decade I have known him. Don, whom I introduced you to in the chapter on the West Side, does yoga, facilitates leadership circles, teaches at Oblate Catholic Seminary, and sports a ponytail. But these uniquely gifted individuals have been my guides for much of the last two decades of my life.

I met Bill for the first time after he read a press release in a Baptist magazine about the launch of THI. He had his team summon me to a meeting in Dallas to hear about my plans. Bill is in a leadership role with the United States Department of Agriculture (USDA), overseeing nutrition programs in the southwest region of the US. When you meet him for the first time and ask him what he does, he responds in his thick Louisiana drawl, "My job is to feed hungry kids."

For our first meeting I drove to Dallas with two colleagues, Suzii Paynter, who was then representing Texas Baptist churches and was the instigator of THI, and JC Dwyer, who works with food banks in Texas, tutored me in all things related to hunger policy, and introduced me to fellow antihunger organizations around the state. JC is a rock star (a cult hero of my staff), and without his help I would likely still be wandering in the wilderness of ignorance. I asked JC and Suzii to attend the meeting with Bill because I honestly felt like I did not know enough to carry on a ten-minute conversation. All I knew was that I wanted to organize the system based on a combination of strategies from the West Side and disaster relief. I thought the approach would be a good complement to all the great work food banks and churches were already doing.

Let's just say Bill was not what I expected. My assumption was that he would be a suited-up bureaucrat who was not interested in what I had to say but was merely keeping tabs on anything new in his region. I thought his staff would be cold and equally uninterested.

When I arrived, his office manager warmly greeted me and told me her son attended Baylor. Bill's director of faith-based initiatives, Leslie, welcomed us to the office with a hug and quickly made a point to tell me about her seminary experience at Howard. Bill walked out of his office in jeans and boots, shook my hand, and said, "Welcome to the USDA, Outlaw!"—a nickname he has called me ever since. I introduced him to my colleagues, and he led us to the meeting, saying, "Come on back to my office. My staff is going to join us to see how we can help you with whatever you need."

Suzii and JC looked at me stunned. I looked back at them stunned. I kept thinking, "He must think I am someone else, someone he is supposed to care about." I think JC and Suzii were thinking the same thing.

Once we sat down in his office, Bill and his team introduced themselves and told us their roles with the USDA. They told us how they had learned about our work and why they wanted to meet. In 2009, the new US president had announced a goal to end childhood hunger and had tasked the USDA with coming up with a plan. The secretary of agriculture had asked his team to begin creating an inventory of ideas, and Bill wanted to hear my pitch.

I told them, "I believe we need to organize a coordinated response on the local, state, and federal levels. Hunger is too large a problem for any one of us to end on our own. It's going to take all of us working together to end it" (though, knowing me, I am sure I was not nearly that concise).

"Outlaw, I love the idea! How can we help?" Bill said.

"I need six months to write up the plan," I told him, "and I could use some help clarifying the USDA's role and better understanding your programs."

"That's it?" Bill responded, a little surprised. "We can certainly help with that." Then nodding toward his team, he told me, "Consider Karen and Leslie at your disposal whenever you need them."

Bill, Suzii, and JC represented several of the largest networks of organizations addressing hunger in Texas. Between the three of them, they were connected to thousands of food pantries, churches, and schools. They had influence with both legislative policy and administrative policy. Their networks became our networks because they believed in the mission of organizing a systemic response to hunger and because they bestowed the trust they had established with their networks onto the work of THI. Through their connections and experience, we began to bring groups and organizations together to the table for dialogue about a coordinated response to end hunger in our state.

Step 3: Plan for Action

Well, I already skipped a critical step, sort of. Really, we just came to it at a later date.

Less than a month after our meeting, Bill called me.

"Hey, Outlaw, are you done yet?"

"Not quite. I was planning to work on this for another six . . ."

He interrupted, "Can you come back up to Dallas next week? We need to prep you because you're gonna present your plan to USDA leadership in Washington, DC."

Confused, I said, "Wait, what?"

Bill responded, "Did you not hear me? I may have a bad connection. I am in my truck headed to my farm."

"No, I think I heard you fine. Thanks for setting up a meeting for us with USDA leadership, but I thought . . ."

He interrupted me again. "Of course. I told them about your plan. They think it could work, but they want to meet you and hear more about it."

The plan was relatively simple, but the execution would be incredibly complex. Our goal was to organize Hunger Free Community Coalitions[1] in communities across the state. These coalitions would organize a strategic response to hunger across organizational and sectoral lines in Texas communities. In Austin, JC and Suzii helped by organizing a Food Policy Roundtable to convene all the state's antihunger advocates so we could have a common agenda and voice while working with the Texas legislature. We also organized a State Operations Team to bring together state agencies administering programs addressing food insecurity. The idea was that THI would serve as the connective tissue among all these groups and would establish and keep communication lines open, a role later described as the backbone role by collective impact theory.

As a bit of background, you might remember that 2009 was the beginning of the Great Recession, and an eager new group of politicians and appointed leaders had just arrived in Washington, DC, ready to solve our country's greatest problems. At the same time, our nation was becoming increasingly fractured. No one wanted to work together in DC or anywhere else. Furthermore, the recession caused hunger to skyrocket. Food insecurity in Texas alone increased by about a million people.

So the complexity of pitching a plan to the USDA to end hunger by working together across ideological and sectoral lines was not lost on me. That is why Bill's response was so puzzling. My training in the urban centers of America had taught me that people like Bill did not care about the end users of their programs. I believed bureaucrats to be coldhearted pragmatists who had the resources to solve big problems but lacked the initiative. Maybe that is true in some cases, but Bill was not like that at all. He seemed to operate from a place of abundance rather than of scarcity. After all, we were not winning the fight against hunger and poverty as a nation, and I think he knew we needed more help. He knew we needed a coordinated response.

Within a few months I was en route to DC. Bill had set up meetings with the USDA's senior brass, and they had set up meetings with industry leaders from the corporate and non-profit advocacy sectors. Everywhere we went I made my pitch: "Hunger is too big and too complex for any of us to address by ourselves; we have to work together in a coordinated effort if we are going to beat this thing."

The USDA team liked the idea. One senior member told me why he liked it. He had been a state administrator in many states throughout his career, most of them blue states or more progressive culturally. He told me that often blue state responses to hunger and poverty do not translate well to red states. He said, "Blue states see addressing hunger and poverty as a core part of the function of government. But red states don't see it that way. They often want congregations and nonprofits to be first responders and see the government as a last resort. So if government is going to engage hunger in red states, it has to be effective and efficient, but most importantly, it has to include the public and the private sectors working together." That was quite an observation. He went on to say, "Blue states will like this too. They are all about efficiency and certainly want to be effective. Can you try this out in other states?"

Step 2: Establish a Coalition Structure

My community development upbringing in the justice movement had taught me that corporations and government were not to be trusted. Bill and his colleagues were already exposing that way of thinking to be false. As a people, we are incredibly gifted at demonizing sectors of society that we rarely, if ever, come in contact with. That was certainly true of much of my experience with government employees.

In 2010, THI hosted our first hunger summit, Together at the Table, at Baylor University. This was Bill's idea. His intent was to convene leaders from across Texas who were addressing hunger to hear our grand plan to be more collaborative—to address the problem of hunger from the bottom up, from the top down, from side to side, and from any other way we knew to address the problem.

To make the summit happen, we had monthly planning meetings with state leaders and government employees to discuss what we hoped to accomplish with the summit, what sessions needed to be offered, and who needed to be invited. The people on the planning team became the core group of individuals representing sectors and organizations on the Food Policy Roundtable and the State Operations Team. At the beginning of one of our planning sessions, my colleague Beth asked for people to introduce themselves and to tell us why they work on the issue of hunger. Admittedly, I did not like the idea of asking these accomplished leaders why they were doing this work. It seemed like a social-worky type of question they would roll their eyes at. But we went with it.

Everyone found their seats around the rectangular grouping of tables. There was an obvious rift between groups—members of nonprofits advocacy organizations sat on one side of the tables and the government employees on the other. Government employees felt the advocacy groups were always judging them for not doing enough. And the advocates felt government employees were never doing enough. The room felt cold and a bit tense when Beth asked her question.

The first person to speak introduced herself and said her faith had led her to want to address hunger. Then the next, "My faith." Then the next, "My faith." This happened over and over again as we went around a room of twenty to thirty leaders. I was shocked. They were shocked. Beth took it in stride like she knew what they would say all along. Immediately, tense shoulders began to relax, and laughter started to fill the room. These leaders were beginning to find points of commonality. They were all there because they wanted to end hunger in Texas. Many of them came to that place because of a faith experience. We had all showed up as individuals representing our respective organizations, but we were becoming a team across agencies and sectors. Hunger wasn't going to stand a chance!

My preconceived notions were continually challenged throughout this process, and I really was beginning to see the common humanity we all shared—from community members to scholars to politicians. We were all created in God's image, and most of us wanted to do good with our lives. By working together, we would achieve the multiplier effect.

Step 1: Recruit (More) Participants

The Great Recession hit our country hard. The poor became poorer, and nonprofits were struggling. The recession also had a major impact on philanthropic gifts to nonprofits to meet the needs of desperate members of our communities. Bill said, "Outlaw, we're gonna have to figure out profit-driven solutions to addressing hunger. Our model right now is too dependent on money that is rarely there when you need it most. I want you to meet with the corporate folks to find out what we can do. There's a group called the Corporate Coalition Against Hunger that I am going to send you to. I will get the folks up in Washington to set up some meetings for you."

This request was pushing the boundaries of my biases. I had recently come to grips with government bureaucrats being in politics to do good, but I had proudly protested against corporate interests in my twenties, so Bill's latest request was really outside of my comfort zone of preconceived notions. Bill was wise enough to know that when I said it would take all of us working together to end hunger, that it actually meant *all* of us. He knew we needed profit-driven solutions so we wouldn't be overly dependent on philanthropic dollars, and we needed to learn more about logistics. He also knew that I needed to confront another bias, and he knew right where to send me: corporate America!

For the first time in my life, I resonated with the story of Jonah. "Lord, send me anywhere but there!"

I went to DC to meet with the leaders of the corporate coalition, and—at the risk of sounding like a broken record—they were not what I expected. They had taken jobs in the corporate sector to address social inequity because of their faith experiences. They had studied business at some of the top universities in the country but wanted to use their business and logistical capabilities to address hunger and poverty in the US and around the globe. They had taken jobs with top US companies because these companies were giving away billions of dollars annually, and they wanted to shape companies from the inside to develop profit-driven strategies to reduce hunger and poverty—and they were succeeding. They were leading the way within their companies to raise wage rates for low-skilled workers, add health-care benefits, provide tuition benefits to send employees to college, and offer job-training opportunities to help employees climb the managerial ladder. Some of these people had a long way to go because their companies were doing more harm than good, but there they were, being faithful witnesses of loving their neighbor within their companies.

"Dang it, Bill! Let me keep some of my biases intact!"

Many of my colleagues in hunger and poverty work believe that nonprofits need to detangle themselves from corporate support. I can understand why. Some corporations do have harmful manufacturing practices, pay poverty wages, and constantly look to make wealthy shareholders wealthier at the expense of the common good. But many corporations are also doing good, and when we cut out an entire sector that employs millions of people from being part of a solution, we are doing the common good a great disservice. Bill was right. It is going to take *all* of us being committed to justice for the hungry and poor if we are going to achieve our goal.

My colleagues from the corporate sector became my tutors in logistics and in developing sustainable business models (something I wish I had learned while running the coffee shop in San Antonio). They helped me see that low-income households are transient, but low-income neighborhoods are not. They said that hunger in the US is largely a logistical problem, and they wanted to work with us to solve it.

When I returned to Texas, I asked my friend and a former marine, Mike, how many meals he missed when he was fighting in the war in Iraq. Mike's marine battalion was among the first to encounter the insurgency in Iraq, so he spent most of his time there chasing them or being chased by them, with bullets flying overhead. Mike responded with a puzzled look, as if to say, "What the heck are you talking about?" "How many meals did I miss?" he asked. "None. A hungry marine is a dead marine."

I said, "So you are telling me that you didn't miss any meals while you were continuously being shot at?"

"Yep. Logistics, man."

If Mike and his platoon didn't miss meals and Amazon can deliver a package to Antarctica, then surely with the surplus of food in America we can solve the problem of hunger. After all, low-income households may be transient but low-income neighborhoods are not. The corporate sector's engagement in our work brought one more party to the table, creating a well-rounded public and private response to food insecurity. Now we needed to take our plan to local communities to see if the model could work.

Step 4: Take Action

For three years, Bill and I, with a number of other state leaders, drove across the state of Texas, holding town hall meetings to organize hunger coalitions. The energy and excitement were infectious. We hired staff to work from our Waco office to try to keep up with the demand of communities, school districts, and even other states wanting to move forward with our Hunger Free Community Coalition model.

However, three years on the road is exhausting. I didn't know how Bill was holding up, but I didn't think I could keep going at that rate. Each December, Bill and I would meet to discuss our plans for the next year and reflect on the past year's accomplishments and opportunities for improvement. When we got together in 2011, he said, "Hey, Outlaw, I am worn-out. I hate to let you down, but I don't think I can keep traveling like we have been."

I laughed and responded, "That is so good to hear. I was feeling like I couldn't keep this thing going either. So how should we move forward in 2012?"

As we talked for a while, I was reminded of the Students for Nonviolent Coordinating Committee of the civil rights era. They created an organizing model they called incarnational organizing. The idea was that civil rights organizers would live in the communities where they registered people to vote in order to strengthen trust and to forge collaborative efforts. That was our path forward. Instead of working completely out of Waco, we would open regional offices that would be the hubs for our work across the state. They would become de facto learning laboratories for our Hunger Free Community Coalition model, and we could share what we learned there with other states and partner agencies across the country.

This was a good plan—but an expensive one. In order to open offices across the great state of Texas, I would have to raise more money than I ever had. Fortunately, the timing was right. National organizations such as Share Our Strength and the Corporate Coalition Against Hunger were ready to invest in innovative, collaborative partnerships to reduce food insecurity, and Texas was on the top of everyone's list. Within a year we had offices from the Panhandle to the Rio Grande Valley and from El Paso to Houston ready to equip surrounding communities to address hunger. Soon our new team members began building relationships in their communities and taking people through the steps of creating coalitions to address hunger and poverty.

Our El Paso staff received a call from a young man named Jesús and his coworkers. They lived west of El Paso in the desert town of Anthony, a town literally split by the Texas, New Mexico, and Mexico borders. Jesús told us that many people in Anthony lived in poverty and some places in town didn't even have running water—much less any industry. Jesús worked for the school district and knew children needed meals during the summer months, but housing in Anthony was very spread out in this rural and mountainous area, so it was hard to reach people. Furthermore, the USDA's summer meal program required meals be eaten by children in a congregant setting at a designated, preapproved location. He also said that teens needed summer employment to provide much-needed income for households and to keep them out of trouble.

Our THI team from El Paso, led by Ruben and Daniel, had already worked with Jesús on breakfast in the classroom. Throughout this process, Ruben and Daniel had developed trust with residents in Anthony and had helped the district double participation in the program. This had made a dramatic impact on academic performance and income for the schools, allowing them to fix up their cafeterias and offer higher quality food. Naturally, when Jesús wanted to address summer hunger for the children of his community, he turned to Ruben and Daniel.

Ruben called our research team at Baylor for advice. We decided this would be the perfect opportunity to leverage our new friends in the corporate sector and pair them with Baylor researchers from our business school who had backgrounds in supply chain logistics, marketing, and so forth. Team member Dr. Kathy Krey convened the masterminds. Many of them flew out to meet with Jesús, who introduced them to the community and drove them around to help them get a feel for the challenges he was facing.

Walmart offered to pay for the research and to provide logistical support. Our faculty, led by Dr. Krey and Dr. Jeff Tanner, began to collect data and work up a plan. After a long assessment period, they came up with a solution. Jesús could hire high school students to help supply lunches to students during the summer months. He hired dozens of kids and split them into two shifts. The first shift came in early in the morning and made food for two thousand lunches daily. Then, working in pairs, the students took coolers of food, loaded them on a bus, and then delivered the food. A bus driver dropped off a pair of students and a cooler at different summer meal sites located at churches, recreation centers, baseball and soccer fields, and apartment complexes around the Texas, Mexico, and New Mexico borders. The students were at their sites for exactly two hours. By the time the last pair was dropped off, it was time to pick up the first pair. The process took four hours round trip and flowed seamlessly.

The route was designed using route optimization techniques popularized by companies like UPS. The process was fuel and time efficient and gave the high school students working for Jesús the right amount of time to serve the children coming to their sites. By the time the students returned to the school where the meals were being prepared, the second shift was ready to load up the bus and do it all over again for dinner, ensuring the children of Anthony received two meals a day. In total, Jesús and his workers served four thousand meals to hungry children daily. Jesus once fed five thousand people in a deserted place, but Jesús did it *every day*.

The program was effective and efficient and had multiple benefits: employment for high school students, resources for the district, and food for the hungry. We could not have come up with a solution by ourselves. We needed to be guided by Jesús and his community. We needed our friends in the corporate sector and faculty researchers to lend their gifts for the cause of the hungry. Together, this group of compassionate masterminds loved their neighbors in a twenty-first-century, big-data kind of way.

Step 5: Assess Progress

One of the things I loved about Jesús's model in Anthony was that he incorporated kids in his district to serve kids in his district. It was one of the closest experiences I have had working to address hunger that mirrored the empowered and empowering community development world of the West Side. Unfortunately, most of our approaches to addressing hunger in America resemble the bread lines of the 1920s. When you pull up to a food pantry, you often see long lines of people wrapped around the building, waiting for their number to be called so they can receive their allotment of free food. This can be a humiliating process, even when the community volunteers are gracious and kind.

The summer meal program provides food for children, but they must eat it at a meal site and cannot take food home. This works well at summer camps, but for children not involved in a summer program, it often means parents bringing their children to a school or church and then watching their children eat, because parents are not allowed food unless they purchase it. Some sites will find ways to engage the parents and often have grant money or use money from a church missions budget to pay for parent meals, giving them at least the dignity of eating with their children. But it still can be a sad scene—watching parents quietly engage their child in conversation as the kids eat their meals, while occasionally giving volunteers a look of gratitude cloaked in absolute humiliation.

If we are going to put in the energy and the effort to attempt to end hunger, we might as well take the extra step of creating a systemic response that is empowering, a response that creates job opportunities and values human dignity, like the one in Anthony.

As we have assessed our progress over the past decade, we reflect with pride that one hundred million more meals are being served annually to Texas children than in 2009. I am proud that more than 350 million breakfasts have been served to Texas children in the past six years simply because the location of breakfast at school was changed. Over five thousand summer meal sites now exist, and food for children during the summer has become a priority for communities across Texas. I could go on and on about the work of our team and our partners. But none of this would have happened without us working together for change. It would not have happened by merely shaming people into working for the common good. It happened because we appealed to the best in all of us—that which reflects our common createdness.

Though we have made major strides, we still have a long way to go. Hunger and poverty are pervasive in Texas, and inequity is extreme around our country. The irony is not lost on me that, in my own community, small farmers struggle to make a living while millions of dollars flow through the local economy in school lunch programs. How can we, like Jesús, create jobs for people needing work while simultaneously solving the hunger crisis? How can the food we serve to the elderly and to our children be the healthiest available to us to ensure a better life for our nation's most vulnerable citizens? As much as we have learned and accomplished, there is still so much more that we need to learn and do.

To put opportunity in perspective, the amount of funding available to the greater Waco community to fund four of the USDA's child nutrition programs—school breakfasts, school lunches, after-school meals, and summer meals—is well over $25 million. Often, as in this case, nearly half the money allotted for food goes unspent. This happens because mayors and council members, school board members and administrators, parents and others do not know this money is available to address food insecurity in their communities. But it does exist, and millions of dollars can provide a lot of food for food-insecure children and create a lot of job opportunities in the food industry—making meals, delivering meals, storing food, and growing food. Those are jobs that cannot be outsourced or at least do not need to be.

Now I know some of you are asking, "If we do not spend this money, can we reduce the federal deficit?" I wish that were the case. Money that is unspent in one area becomes tax breaks for companies in other areas. When this money is spent at the local level to provide food and jobs, however, it creates more taxpayers, who in turn fund our schools, roads, and first responders. I can't imagine a more noble way for our nation to spend tax dollars than to feed the hungry, and the idea of a small farmer from my community being the center point of that activity, rather than someone standing in a bread line waiting for a handout, sounds like the kingdom of God to me.

All that said, we have many opportunities to continue to address the crisis of hunger, and with creative problem solving and a collaborative approach, I am looking forward to seeing what emerges in the next decade.

Lolita's Lessons on Leadership for Social Change

When Amy and I lived on the World Hunger Relief farm in 2003 for a one-year residential internship, we (the farm) bought a donkey to keep coyotes away from the sheep. I knew that donkeys make good pack animals, but I learned they are also fiercely loyal to a herd and vicious with coyotes. We decided to name our new donkey Lolita after our favorite taco shop in town.

Lolita did her job. Any approaching coyotes would be run off or stomped into the ground. Every morning Lolita would wail at me as I walked up, as if she were bragging about the previous evening's adventures and, of course, demanding her well-earned breakfast.

We grazed the land rotationally, meaning we never kept a herd in one place for too long. The season was changing, which meant it was time to move the sheep and goats into the north pasture for the winter and for Lolita to move with them.

There is typically a reason for old sayings. "Stubborn as a mule" came to mind that morning. Lolita gladly walked to the edge of the east pasture with us, but she would go no farther. She looked at us as if to smirk and say, "This ain't happening." The farm manager, Brad, and I looked at each other, then we looked at her. I swear to you I think I heard that donkey laugh at us.

Naturally, we tried the lead rope first. She didn't budge. So both of us tried pulling her with the lead rope. She still didn't budge, but her smirk began to turn to agitation. Brad tried pulling her while I pushed from behind. Not only did she not move an inch forward, but she also started to buck a little, so I decided to end that plan before she did to me what she did to coyotes.

Unlike me, Brad was a real farmer. Don't get me wrong, I loved farming. I especially enjoyed communing with the animals, but I wasn't very good at it. Brad, the real farmer, started getting frustrated, because he knew how much we needed to accomplish that day. We needed to get all the animals moved into the north pasture, and Lolita's obstinance was taking up too much time.

So Brad got the tractor. We may not have been strong enough to move Lolita, but our old John Deere sure was. We tied Lolita's lead rope to the back of the tractor, and Brad started to drive. Lolita tried to brace herself but wasn't successful, so she just sat down. All of a sudden, the tractor was dragging Lolita, our prize coyote fighter. Brad stopped the tractor immediately. We needed Lolita to be healthy, and dragging her would have left her bleeding and bruised. So we untied her and sat there bewildered, trying to figure out what to do.

Then one of us remembered (let's say it was me because I am writing this book) the old farmer we bought her from saying that when we needed to lead her, we should put the lead rope behind her and gently put pressure on her backside. Then she would think she was leading us and would walk right where we wanted her to go. Sure enough, we put the lead rope behind Lolita's backside, and she proudly led us to the north pasture.

Brad and I just shook our heads and laughed. Lolita would occasionally look back at us to make sure we were following her lead until she arrived unscathed in the lush north pasture.

As I reflect back on much of my work addressing hunger and poverty, it is not lost on me that people like Bill and Don have been doing the same thing to me. Like that old donkey, I have been stubborn, hardheaded, and too often insistent on leading if I was going to go anywhere or address anything, regardless of whether I knew anything. I am grateful that they at least let me think I was leading.

I am also grateful that our work together has produced fruit and lots of it. THI is an experiment. Can we find common ground for the common good? Can we address hunger and poverty systemically? Can Democrats and Republicans work together? Our world has grown more contentious over the last decade, and our politicians are spewing hateful things I never thought I would hear from our representatives—least of all from a president—but there is still hope. There is hope because we are created by and in the image of a God who loves all of us. There is hope because there are people across this nation committed to justice for the poor. There is hope because our Creator lives among us and inside us, giving us strength when we have none and bounty in deserted places. So, yes, we can end hunger systemically, and there is much fertile common ground still waiting to be cultivated by us that will yield more justice for the poor, the hungry, the immigrant.

Jesus told us, "The harvest is plentiful, but the laborers are few" (Matt. 9:37). We can end hunger and poverty, but only if *you* come join the harvest.

<del>10</del>

JUSTICE

Our Cultural Moment to Find
Common Ground for the Common Good

15th Street

The house I lived in on 15th Street during seminary had a number of issues, and plumbing was its arch nemesis. If we ran the kitchen faucet, took a shower, or flushed the toilet, we could hear water splash beneath the house. It was as disgusting as it sounds. We called our landlord repeatedly to send a plumber over, but he ignored our calls. The problem became so bad that water began seeping out from under our house into the front yard. A police officer patrolling the neighborhood for drugs and prostitution noticed it and threatened to have us fined if we didn't do something about it. When we alerted our landlord to this, he finally sent someone over to check out the problem.

The plumber arrived a few days later and crept through the crawl space beneath our hallway built for a hobbit-sized person.

We could hear his groans from underneath the house as he assessed the situation. He reemerged after less than a half hour and called our landlord to report the news. He would need to completely redo the pipes underneath the house—a costly conclusion to an ever-stinky problem.

After speaking to the landlord on the phone, the plumber left to get supplies to begin overhauling our pipes—or so we thought. When he returned, he didn't have new pipes with him. Instead, he had round concrete steps that he placed throughout the front yard so we would not have to step in the sludge.

Concrete steps! That was our landlord's solution to our plumbing problem.

The police officer returned the following week and assessed the landlord's "solution" to our problem. He may have been more aggravated than we were. We relayed the officer's frustration to our landlord, who reluctantly agreed to send the plumber back to the house to overhaul the pipes.

The concrete steps likely prevented us from getting sick from walking through sewage on our way to and from our home, but they were not a good long-term solution. The only viable long-term solution was to fix the pipes. If the landlord had refused to do so, his decision eventually would have been catastrophic for his investment property because the city would have red tagged it, forcing the landlord to tear down the house. The landlord had to pay to fix the pipes or his investment in the home would have become a significant loss.

When we address only symptoms of a larger problem, doing so can be lifesaving in the moment, but it does not get us to an actual long-term solution. Hunger and poverty won't fix themselves, just like the pipes weren't going to fix themselves. They require us to do the dirty work of crawling underneath the house to identify the root causes of the problem and working together to fix it. Whether our responsibility is creating a plan for a Hunger Free Community Coalition in our city or finding common ground among politicians and advocates in Washington, DC, we must work together to create a systemic response to hunger and poverty, otherwise the problem will persist.

Talcott Parsons, whom I referenced earlier, wrote about systems his entire life—from family systems to cultural systems. He noted that a strong system often needs what he called tension maintenance.[1] A little tweak here or there can often make all the difference. But he noted (as did all the biblical prophets) that if countries refuse to do appropriate tension maintenance, they pass the point for reform and are often thrust into upheaval.[2] When that happens, the system completely breaks down and the poor and the rich alike are sent into a tailspin. Essentially, fix the plumbing now or tear down the entire house later.

Patron Saints of Social Change

If there was a patron saint of cultivating common ground for the common good, it was the British parliamentarian William Wilberforce. Motivated by his Christian faith, Wilberforce addressed the injustice of the British slave trade during his tenure in Parliament in the late 1700s. He cultivated a coalition of the willing by sowing seeds of trust among members of Parliament, former slave traders, the wealthy and powerful, Christians, humanists, and so on.[3] His coalition successfully ended the slave trade just days before Wilberforce died. He quite literally gave his life to the cause.

But as one biographer noted, Wilberforce's greatest accomplishment was not ending the British slave trade but ending the very *idea* that slavery was an acceptable form of commerce.[4] Slavery had existed for almost all of human history. Slavery was a part of the normal human condition, a part of the normal economic condition for thousands of years of human history. Who did Wilberforce think he was to tear at the economic fabric woven together since the beginning of time? He was dismantling one of the critical pillars to creating wealth. This radical idea was equal to proposing that the world was not flat but round. It is amazing that he lived to see this through and was not assassinated merely for proposing this idea in the British Parliament. But Wilberforce's powerful notion forever transformed how we view economic conditions.

Each period in human history provides an opportunity to advance society. Sometimes that advancement is through new scientific discovery or philosophical ways of seeing the world. Sometimes critical moments in history reframe how we see fellow humans. Seeing slaves as people created in God's image had historical reverberations still being felt today. Anytime slavery is mentioned in the modern context, society immediately judges it as wrong. Christians quickly point to it as cultural sin.

It was not always this way. I was raised Southern Baptist. Baptists in America split over slavery. Southern Baptists believed missionaries could be slave holders, and Northern Baptists did not. So we split. Fast-forward two centuries. I have never once heard in my time in Southern Baptist churches in the '70s, '80s, and '90s that slavery should be reintroduced. That is because Wilberforce promoted the notions that slaves were created in God's image, they were human beings, and the creation of wealth had no business being done on the backs of slaves. This was not an overnight realization, of course. It took centuries to eventually change our collective consciousness, but it happened. Ending the *idea* that slavery was an acceptable form of commerce was history altering.

Close to a hundred and fifty years after Wilberforce, Dr. King and civil rights activists caused society to advance again, this time on the issue of race. Again, many people of our nation, including people of faith, held the belief that we were not all created equal, that people of color were not as human as those of Anglo origins. This justified actions such as segregation, lynching, paying unlivable wages to people of color, and so on. civil rights leaders, in turn, challenged the idea of this inherent inequality, changing the American consciousness about racism and equality. This too was a history-altering time. The world will never be the same because of it. Even though racism is still pervasive in our nation today, it is widely seen as sinful because of the efforts of activists during the civil rights era. People of color are not a degradation; people who hold racist beliefs have degraded ways of seeing the world.

Now we are faced with another moment of historical significance. The richest nation in the history of the world has over forty million people experiencing hunger and poverty. Inner cities, rural communities, and *colonías* have little hope of economic vitality. The poor have no political or economic power to help themselves in their quest to provide adequate food for their families, and some children are forced to dig through dumpsters to find something to eat when school is out. Furthermore, what used to be a bipartisan issue to address human need has been replaced with political and theological bickering and blaming the poor for their plight. This partisan divide reaching all the way to the pews in our churches has further disintegrated our spirit of cooperation and our ability to problem solve with our neighbor. We are certainly in a deserted place.

In the story of the feeding of the five thousand in the Gospel of Luke, the disciples come to Jesus in a deserted place. There is no food to be found. So the disciples resort to an ideology of personal responsibility. After all, resources are scarce in the desert. But Jesus will have none of it. "You give them something to eat."

The miracle happens in the desert through the generosity of someone sharing *all* the food he had. The risk here is minimalized, but someone, a child, gave up all of his food without the foreknowledge that a miracle would in turn provide amply for him.

Wilberforce and King did the same. They gave up all they had to shine a light on the injustices of slavery and racism that were rooted in a lack of acknowledgment that we are all created in God's image. That was the root of the issue in both contexts, and that lack of acknowledgment created profound injustices that wounded our world in ways we may never fully heal from.

But their courage to act and their commitment to the cause of their day changed the world forever.

Likewise, in our time we must end the *idea* that hunger and poverty are acceptable socioeconomic conditions. I fundamentally believe we do not see the poor as our equals, as created in the image of God, just as we are. If we did, how could we justify their going without food, clothing, and shelter? If we saw the poor as human, how could we justify the treatment of the immigrant mother separated from her child at the border? How could we justify wage rates that don't allow someone to buy their own food or medication or to provide for their families, just as we hope to provide for our families? We must admit to ourselves that we do not see the homeless man on the corner as being created in the image of the same God who created us. If we think the poor are created in God's image, then how can we justify poverty? How can we justify children going without food?

In Matthew 25, Jesus radically calls the "least of these" his brothers and sisters—members of his family, not servants, slaves, or subjects. They are his brothers and sisters, those whose destinies are interwoven with his own. The imperative of the Christian is to feed the hungry, visit the sick, and provide a place for the stranger. It is only by doing these things that one receives the inheritance of the kingdom.

This is our time to recognize the createdness of all of our brothers and sisters, no matter their socioeconomic level, their ethnicity, where they live, or where they are from. Just as we did with slavery, we must alter history with the idea that hunger and poverty are not required human conditions.

Rather than simply asking, "Will this create more wealth?" we must make our economic decisions—including those regarding food, shelter, wages, trade and tax policy, education policy, health care, and so on—based on this litmus test: "Will this create more poverty or reduce it?"

Hunger and poverty are not inevitable by-products of economic and social systems unless we intentionally create systems to exploit our brothers and sisters. We the people are not and have never been a passive people. We face our problems head-on, and hunger and poverty are a humanitarian crisis we have the capacity to address.

Our Hope

Our Christian faith tradition warns us of systemic oppression of the poor. Scripture is full of moral imperatives about the ways Jesus's followers are to treat the poor and hungry in the world.

As Christians, faith animates our worldview. We believe that people are created in the image of God; therefore, we are all inherently equal. We believe that loving our neighbor as ourselves means we are mutually responsible for one another. We believe that an expression of this mutual responsibility is to ensure that all people have enough food to live an active, healthy lifestyle. As Paul puts it, "I do not mean that there should be relief for others and pressure on you, but it is a question of a fair balance between your present abundance and their need, so that their abundance may be for your need, in order that there may be fair balance. As it is written: 'The one who had much did not have too much, and the one who had little did not have too little'" (2 Cor. 8:13–15).

We can have hope in this deserted time in human history when food insecurity is rampant and we are more polarized than ever before, because God moves in the desert when we join with him.

America's great experiment has taken us through some dark periods in our history. For some of us, the slogan "Make America Great Again" harkens back to the postwar optimism of the greatest generation. For many others, such as American citizens of color, that phrase conjures painful memories of slavery, segregation, and long hours of manual labor with very little compensation.

Making America great for everyone means we can't wait until we agree with one another on everything. We have to find common ground in order to bring humanitarian relief to our own domestic disaster of poverty and hunger. Without integrated systems of response, we will repeat the chaos of Hurricane Katrina, and without recognizing our common humanity and finding common ground, we will pass the point of reform and spin out more violent clashes like we saw in Ferguson and Charlottesville. Either we become catalysts in the movement for justice or we stand by and allow the perpetuation of injustice to provoke unrest and violence.

Faith-based communities have often been at the forefront of grassroots change in this country. The kingdom of God gives churches a vision and a mandate for standing with the hungry and the impoverished—for loving our neighbor as we love ourselves.

How we go about this change is of the utmost importance. We must be committed to the principles of nonviolent social change; otherwise, we embody the injustices we are working so hard to overcome. Cultivating trust, collaboration, and commitment to the cause are our mantras toward that prophetic end. These principles will guide us to lasting, sustainable change, the means of which are as just as the ends we seek.

Granddaddy and the Civil Rights Movement

I love documentaries. I can binge-watch stories about the Roosevelts, the Lincolns, the Dust Bowl, and so on. Each year the *Eyes on the Prize* documentary typically runs during Black History Month. And almost every year I sit down to watch the story of the civil rights movement as if I have never seen it before.

When the documentary culminates with the images of Bull Conner and the Birmingham police turning fire hoses on African American children protesting in Birmingham's Kelly Ingram Park, I cannot help but think that the people of that generation are judged by history based on whose side they were on that day. Were they on the side of the children protesting for equal rights or on the side of Bull Conner and the Birmingham police officers? Each generation is judged based on what they do or do not do to further the cause of justice. For that generation, the cause was civil rights.

Like many of us who were born after that time, I wonder what side my family members were on. I can only imagine that many of my white, southern-born family members were on the side of Bull Conner. That is a sin my family members and I must carry with us.

On the occasion of my grandfather's funeral, I was gratified to hear about a bright spot in our family history from my uncle. Prior to moving to Springhill, Granddaddy was a Baptist pastor in southern Arkansas in the mid-1960s. His congregation was exclusively white in a very rural area near the Arkansas-Louisiana border. One Wednesday evening after church, my grandfather, my grandmother (Mama Ruth), my father, and his sister (Janie) were traveling home when they saw a large fire on the horizon. As they got closer to the flames, they realized the fire was in the front yard of an African American family who lived near my grandparents' home. They could see something in the middle of the flames but couldn't make it out until they got within a few yards of the house. It was a cross. The fire was billowing from it as if the perpetrators wanted people to see it all the way up in Little Rock.

My granddad parked his old Buick and jumped out of the car. He ran into the yard and began looking around to see if the Klansmen were still on the property. When he realized they had gone, he told my father to go inside to check on the family while he put out the fire. My father went inside to find children huddled up in the back room of the house, terrified. Their parents were away at work.

My grandfather put out the fire and then walked to the edge of the yard and peered into the woods across the street. He knew the Klansmen were likely watching everything from the safety of the forest. He yelled at them, "Cowards! Cowards! Come out! How can you use the symbol of love as a symbol of hate?"

The Klansmen never came out.

Many of the Klansmen likely attended my grandfather's church. Some of them were probably deacons. He could have let fear rule that evening and passed on by that home for the safety of his. But he didn't. In that moment, like the child who gave all of his food to Jesus, my granddad gave all he cared about, risking his safety and that of his family, to confront the evil of injustice.

My grandfather's generation was judged based on what they did or did not do to further the cause of civil rights. I believe our generation will be judged based on what we do or do not do to further the cause of those living in hunger and poverty in our world.

With over forty million Americans experiencing food insecurity and likely many other poverty-related issues—such as poor housing, low-paying jobs, failing schools, a lack of access to health care, neighborhoods marked by violence, and the highest level of economic inequality in the developed world—we are a nation in crisis. As Wilberforce said to the House of Commons in 1791, "You may choose to look the other way, but you can never again say that you did not know."[5]

Hunger in our modern American context is not about famine or a lack of production but about a lack of concerted effort to ensure that people have access to food. People without access to food are our scapegoats. They are a people without political power. Simply put, they are the people Jesus instructs us to look after, because our mutual well-being requires it.

The calling of the faithful is clear: feed the hungry. If we do, then on our final day may we hear Jesus say to us, "Come, you that are blessed by my Father, inherit the kingdom prepared for you from the foundation of the world; for I was hungry and you gave me food" (Matt. 25:34–35).

NOTES

Chapter 1: Disaster

1. "Food Security Status of US Households in 2017," United States Department of Agriculture, 2017, https://www.ers.usda.gov/webdocs/publications/90023/err-256.pdf?v=0.

2. Feeding America, "Map the Meal Gap: Food Insecurity in the United States 2016," 2018, http://map.feedingamerica.org/.

3. M. Eugene Boring, "The Gospel of Matthew," in *The New Interpreter's Bible Commentary*, ed. Leander E. Keck (Nashville: Abingdon Press, 1995), 8:455.

4. Boring, "Gospel of Matthew," 8:455.

5. Boring, "Gospel of Matthew," 8:456.

6. John Kania and Mark Kramer, "Collective Impact," *Stanford Social Innovation Review* (Winter 2011), https://ssir.org/articles/entry/collective_impact.

7. Kania and Kramer, "Collective Impact."

Chapter 2: Broken Streetlights

1. Names have been changed to protect anonymity.

2. Franklin Delano Roosevelt, "One Third of a Nation: FDR's Second Inaugural Address," January 20, 1937. Transcript available at http://historymatters.gmu.edu/d/5105/.

3. Dan Kopf, "Embarrassment of Riches: Trump's First Seventeen Cabinet-Level Picks Have More Money Than a Third of American Households Combined" December 15, 2016, https://qz.com/862412/trumps-16-cabinet-level-picks-have-more-money-than-a-third-of-american-households-combined/.

4. "The policies or principles of any of various political parties that seek to represent the interests of ordinary people, *spec.* of the Populists of the US or Russia." Also "support for or representation of ordinary people or

their views; speech, action, writing, etc. intended to have general appeal." OED Online, July 2018, Oxford University Press, http://www.oed.com/view /Entry/147930.

5. This is King's paraphrasing of a portion of a sermon delivered in 1853 by the abolitionist minister Theodore Parker.

Chapter 3: A Priest and a Prostitute

1. I learned later that the movie is the classic biopic of St. Francis of As- sisi, *Brother Son, Sister Moon*, directed by Franco Zeffirelli (Hollywood, CA: Paramount Pictures, 1972).

2. A more thorough account of the life of St. Francis can be found in Donald Spoto, *The Reluctant Saint: The Life of Francis of Assisi* (New York: Viking, 2002).

3. Taylor Branch, *Parting the Waters: America in the King Years 1954–63* (New York: Simon & Schuster, 1988), 756.

4. As I later learned, over five hundred thousand people are homeless on any given night in the United States. Meghan Henry, Azim Shivji, Tanya de Sousa, et al., "The 2015 Annual Homeless Assessment Report (AHAR) to Congress, Part 1: Point-in-Time Estimates of Homelessness," Novem- ber 19, 2015, https://www.abtassociates.com/insights/publications/report /the-2015-annual-homeless-assessment-report-ahar-to-congress-part-1.

5. As social justice reformer Walter Rauschenbusch once wrote, "The better we know Jesus, the more social do his thoughts and aims become." Walter Rauschenbusch, *Christianity and the Social Crisis* (New York: Mac- millan, 1913), 46.

6. About 30 percent of people who are chronically homeless have mental health conditions. "Current Statistics on the Prevalence and Characteristics of People Experiencing Homelessness in the United States," Substance Abuse and Mental Health Services Administration, July 2011, https://www.samhsa.gov /sites/default/files/programs_campaigns/homelessness_programs_resources /hrc-factsheet-current-statistics-prevalence-characteristics-homelessness.pdf.

7. To complicate issues with mental health, almost 35 percent of the homeless also battle substance abuse. This is often a coping mechanism to deal with extreme mental health problems. See "Current Statistics."

8. Names have been changed to protect anonymity.

9. A convenience sample—a nonprobability sampling method where the sample is take from a group of people easy to contact or to reach—collected by economists Scott Cunningham and Todd Kendall found that while 13 percent of all internet sex workers reported having been physically assaulted by a client, among street prostitutes the number was a staggering 44 percent. Scott Cunningham, personal communication, February 2017. See also John J. Potterat, Devon D. Brewer, Stephen Q. Muth, et al., "Mortality in a Long-term Open Cohort of Prostitute Women," *American Journal of Epidemiology* 159 (2004): 778–85.

10. It is estimated that "6,851,000 persons were under the supervision of US adult correctional systems." Statistics on rearrest rates are grim: "Within three years of release, about two-thirds (67.8 percent) of released prisoners were rearrested. Within five years of release, about three-quarters (76.6 percent) of released prisoners were rearrested." Matthew R. Durose, Alexia D. Cooper, and Howard N. Snyder, "Recidivism of Prisoners Released in 30 States in 2005: Patterns from 2005 to 2010," Bureau of Justice Statistics Special Report, April 2014, NCJ 244205, https://www.bjs.gov/content/pub/pdf/rprts05p0510.pdf.

11. Names have been changed to protect anonymity.

12. For an in-depth explanation and overview of the political philosophy of compassionate conservatism, see Marvin Olasky, *Compassionate Conservatism: What It Is, What It Does, and How It Can Transform America* (New York: Free Press, 2000).

13. See his now-classic text, Gustavo Gutiérrez, *A Theology of Liberation: History, Politics, and Salvation*, 2nd ed. (Maryknoll, NY: Orbis, 1988).

14. Gutiérrez, *A Theology of Liberation*, xxxi.

Chapter 4: The People

1. Names have been changed to protect anonymity.

2. Kayla Fontenot, Jessica Semega, and Melissa Kollar, "Income and Poverty in the United States: 2017," Current Population Reports, September 2018, https://www.census.gov/content/dam/Census/library/publications/2018/demo/p60-263.pdf.

3. Fontenot, Semega, and Kollar, "Income and Poverty in the United States: 2017."

4. Fontenot, Semega, and Kollar, "Income and Poverty in the United States: 2017."

5. Feeding America, "Map the Meal Gap: Food Insecurity in the United States 2016," 2018, http://map.feedingamerica.org/.

6. Feeding America, "Map the Meal Gap."

7. Feeding America, "Map the Meal Gap."

8. Alisha Coleman-Jensen, Matthew P. Rabbitt, Christian A. Gregory, et al., "Household Food Security in the United States in 2016," United States Department of Agriculture, September 2017, https://www.ers.usda.gov/webdocs/publications/84973/err-237.pdf?v=42979.

9. Alisha Coleman-Jensen and Mark Nord, "Food Insecurity among Households with Working-Age Adults with Disabilities," United States Department of Agriculture, January 2013, https://www.ers.usda.gov/webdocs/publications/45038/34589_err_144.pdf?v=41284.

10. Healthy People 2010, "Nutrition and Overweight, Chapter 19," 2011, https://www.cdc.gov/nchs/data/hpdata2010/hp2010_final_review_focus_area_19.pdf.

11. Robynn Cox and Sally Wallace, "The Impact of Incarceration on Food Insecurity among Households with Children," *Andrew Young School of Policy Studies Research Paper Series* 13-05, February 15, 2013, https://papers.ssrn.com/sol3/papers.cfm?abstract_id=2212909&rec=1&srcabs=1515129&alg=7&pos=4.

12. John Cook, "Risk and Protective Factors Associated with Prevalence of VLFS in Children among Children of Foreign-Born Mothers," *University of Kentucky Center for Poverty Research Discussion Series*, August 20, 2013, https://uknowledge.uky.edu/cgi/viewcontent.cgi?article=1011&context=ukcpr_papers.

13. Jung Sun Lee, Craig Gundersen, John Cook, et al., "Food Insecurity and Health Across the Lifespan," *Advances in Nutrition* 3 (2012): 44–74; and Craig Hadley and Deborah L. Crooks, "Coping and the Biosocial Consequences of Food Insecurity in the 21st Century," *American Journal of Physical Anthropology* 55 (2012): 72–94.

14. Coleman-Jensen, Rabbitt, Gregory, et al., "Household Food Security in the United States in 2016."

15. Coleman-Jensen, Rabbitt, Gregory, et al., "Household Food Security in the United States in 2016."

16. Hilary Seligman, Ann Bolger, David Guzman, et al., "Exhaustion of Food Budgets at Month's End and Hospital Admissions for Hypoglycemia," *Health Affairs* 33 (2014): 116–23.

17. Food insecurity is measured by the US Household Food Security Survey Module. "Food Security Status of US Households in 2017," United States Department of Agriculture, 2017, https://www.ers.usda.gov/webdocs/publications/90023/err-256.pdf?v=0.

18. Coleman-Jensen, Rabbitt, Gregory, et al., "Household Food Security in the United States in 2016."

19. Alisha Coleman-Jensen, "Working for Peanuts: Nonstandard Work and Food Insecurity Across Household Structure," *Journal of Family and Economic Issues* 32 (2011): 84–97; and David Autor, "The Growth of Low-skill Service Jobs and the Polarization of the US Labor Market," *American Economic Review* 103 (2013): 1553–97.

20. Names have been changed to protect anonymity.

21. National Commission on Hunger, "Freedom from Hunger: An Achievable Goal for the United States of America, Recommendations of the National Commission on Hunger to Congress and the Secretary of the Department of Agriculture," 2015, https://cybercemetery.unt.edu/archive/hungercommission/20151216222324/https://hungercommission.rti.org/Portals/0/SiteHtml/Activities/FinalReport/Hunger_Commission_Final_Report.pdf.

22. "Public High School Graduation Rates," National Center for Education Statistics, last updated May 2018, http://nces.ed.gov/programs/coe/indicator_coi.asp.

23. Katherine Alaimo, Christine M. Olson, and Edward A. Frongillo Jr., "Food Insufficiency and American School-Aged Children's Cognitive, Academic, and Psychosocial Development," *American Academy of Pediatrics* 108 (2001): 44–53.

24. Coleman-Jensen, Rabbitt, Gregory, et al., "Household Food Security in the United States in 2016."

25. "Highlights of Women's Earnings in 2016," United States Bureau of Labor Statistics, August 2017, https://www.bls.gov/opub/reports/womens -earnings/2016/pdf/home.pdf.

26. Coleman-Jensen, Rabbitt, Gregory, et al., "Household Food Security in the United States in 2016."

27. National Commission on Hunger, "Freedom from Hunger."

28. Brené Brown, *Braving the Wilderness: The Quest for True Belonging and the Courage to Stand Alone* (New York: Random House, 2017). Brené Brown quotes the work of David Smith and Michell Maiese on the topic of dehumanization.

29. Erin Nolen, email correspondence, January 17, 2018.

30. Erin Nolen, email correspondence, January 17, 2018.

31. Erin Nolen, email correspondence, January 17, 2018.

Chapter 5: The Desert

1. "Food Access Research Atlas," United States Department of Agriculture, December 5, 2017, https://www.ers.usda.gov/data-products/food-access -research-atlas/documentation.

2. Estela Alonso, "A Comparison of Children Living in Extreme Urban Poverty Participating in an Enrichment Program with a Control Group on Narrative Skills Using Responses to a Story Telling Task" (honors program thesis, Baylor University, May 2014), https://baylor-ir.tdl.org/baylor-ir/bit stream/handle/2104/8984/FINAL%20THESIS%20pdf.pdf?sequence=1.

3. A description of Maslow's hierarchy can be found at https://www.simply psychology.org/maslow.html.

4. "NSLP Statistics," Texas Department of Agriculture, August 2, 2018, http://squaremeals.org/Programs/NationalSchoolLunchProgram/NSLPSta tistics.aspx.

5. Kathy J. Krey and Erin R. Nolen, "The Effect of Universal-Free School Breakfast on Milk Consumption and Nutrient Intake," *Food Studies: An Interdisciplinary Journal* 5 (2015): 23–33.

6. Krey and Nolen, "Effect of Universal-Free School Breakfast."

7. Krey and Nolen, "Effect of Universal-Free School Breakfast."

8. Texas Hunger Initiative analysis of Texas Department of Agriculture child nutrition program administrative claim data, program years 2009–2018.

9. Name has been changed to protect anonymity.

10. As originally reported in Taylor McKinney, Ashley Yeaman, Rebecca Fortson, et al., "Texas School Breakfast Report Card: 2016 Edition." 2016, https://www.baylor.edu/texashunger/index.php?id=930469.

11. As reported in McKinney, Yeaman, Fortson, et al., "Texas School Breakfast Report Card: 2016 Edition."

12. McKinney, Yeaman, Fortson, et al., "Texas School Breakfast Report Card: 2016 Edition."

13. Name has been changed to protect anonymity.

14. Judith Bartfeld, Craig Gundersen, Timothy M. Smeeding, et al., eds., *SNAP Matters* (Stanford, CA: Stanford University Press, 2016), 1–3.

15. Thomas Ptacek, public testimony before the National Commission on Hunger, Research Triangle Park, NC, July 20, 2015.

16. "Supplemental Nutrition Assistance Program Participation and Costs," United States Department of Agriculture, August 3, 2018, https://fns-prod.azureedge.net/sites/default/files/pd/SNAPsummary.pdf.

17. Mark Zandi, "Assessing the Macro Economic Impact of Fiscal Stimulus 2008," Moody's Economy.com, August 2, 2018, https://www.economy.com/mark-zandi/documents/Stimulus-Impact-2008.pdf.

Chapter 6: Organize

1. Saul Alinsky, *Rules for Radicals: A Pragmatic Primer for Realistic Radicals* (New York: Vintage Books, 1971).

2. Alinsky, *Rules for Radicals*.

3. E. Nolen, J. Everett, and D. McDurham, "Together at the Table," in *Food and Poverty*, ed. L. Hossfeld, B. Kelly, and J. Waity, 179–90 (Nashville: Vanderbilt University Press, 2018).

4. Pat N. Lackey, *Invitation to Talcott Parsons' Theory* (Houston: Cap and Gown Press, 1987).

5. Lackey, *Invitation to Talcott Parsons' Theory*, 95–96.

6. Texas Hunger Initiative, "A Toolkit for Developing and Strengthening Hunger Free Communities," 2018, https://www.baylor.edu/texashunger/index.php?id=953881.

7. Dave Minor, past chair of Indy Hunger Network, email correspondence, April 2018.

8. Taylor Branch, *Parting the Waters: America in the King Years 1954–63* (New York: Simon & Schuster, 1988), 120–42.

9. This story is adapted from Jeremy Everett, "Talcott Parsons," paper submitted for class, Baylor University, January 21, 2016.

Chapter 7: The West Side

1. Martin Luther King Jr., "Letter from Birmingham Jail," June 12, 1963, http://okra.stanford.edu/transcription/document_images/undecided/630416-019.pdf.

Chapter 8: Politics

1. This is Dr. King's paraphrasing of a portion of a sermon delivered in 1853 by the abolitionist minister Theodore Parker.

2. Ezra Klein, "What Obama Would Say at the State of the Union If He Were Being Brutally Honest," *Vox*, January 20, 2015, http://www.vox.com/2015/1/20/7852905/obama-state-of-the-union/.

3. National Commission on Hunger, "Freedom from Hunger: An Achievable Goal for the United States of America, Recommendations of the National Commission on Hunger to Congress and the Secretary of the Department of Agriculture," 2015, https://cybercemetery.unt.edu/archive/hungercommis sion/20151216222324/https://hungercommission.rti.org/Portals/0/SiteHtml /Activities/FinalReport/Hunger_Commission_Final_Report.pdf.

4. Martin Luther King Jr., *Strength to Love* (Cleveland: Collins & World, 1977).

Chapter 9: Together at the Table

1. Note that we called them Food Planning Associations at the time.

Chapter 10: Justice

1. Pat N. Lackey, *Invitation to Talcott Parsons' Theory* (Houston: Cap and Gown Press, 1987), 83–101.

2. Lackey, *Invitation to Talcott Parsons' Theory*, 83–105.

3. Eric Metaxas, *Amazing Grace and the Heroic Campaign to End Slavery* (New York: HarperCollins, 2007).

4. Metaxas, *Amazing Grace*.

5. Metaxas, *Amazing Grace*.

INDEX

abundance, 55
advertising (coalition building), 78
advocacy groups, 124
aging, 48–49
al-Assad, Bashar, 107
Alazan Apache Courts (San Antonio), 86, 90, 102
Alinsky, Saul, 67–69
Alliance to End Hunger, 76
American Indians of Texas-Spanish Colonial Missions, 90
Arispe, Don, 94, 118–19, 134
assessing progress, 82–83, 130–32
asset-based community development, 79, 99–100

baptism, 39
Baptists, 92–94, 139
Baylor University, 129
"bending the universe towards justice," 23, 109
Birmingham, in civil rights movement, 29
blaming the poor, 7, 37
brain development, 57–58
bread lines, 130

broken streetlights, 21–23, 57
brother's keeper, 116
Brother Son, Sister Moon (film), 27–29
Brown, Jim, 26
Burnet County Hunger Coalition, 77
Bush, George W., 38

cartel violence, 113–14
Christian community development, 56, 99–100
Cisneros, Henry, 104
civic leaders, 77
civil rights movement, 48, 128, 139–40, 143–44
Clinton, Bill, 103
Clinton, Hillary, 104
coalition building, 75, 78–79
coffee shop community center. *See* Guadalupe Street Coffee (San Antonio)
collaboration, 11, 81, 128. *See also* trust, collaboration, and commitment
collective impact, 14
college prep programming, 98–99

colonias, 42–43, 140
commitment. *See* trust, collaboration, and commitment
common good, 23, 134
common ground, 23–24, 108–10, 124, 134–35, 138, 143
community assessment, 13, 79
community-based organizations, mission and purpose, 106
community center, 100
community empowerment, 22
community organizing, 67
compassionate conservatism, 149n12
"compassionate conservatives," 38
conflict, 109
confrontation, 69, 110
Conner, Bull, 29, 143–44
consensus, 70, 112
coordinated response, 5–7
Corporate Coalition Against Hunger, 125, 128
corporate sector, 125–27, 129

Dallas Coalition for Hunger Solutions, 74–75, 82
Day of Atonement, 50
dehumanizing the poor, 51–52
Democrats and Republicans, 109, 111, 134
demonizing immigrants, 114
demonizing the other, 108
demonizing the poor, 51
desert, as opportunity, 55
distribution of tasks, 81
Dorrell, Jimmy and Janet, 56–57
dumpster-diving kids, 8–9
Dwyer, JC, 119–20, 121

economic opportunity, 20
education, and hunger, 46–47
elites, 69
Excellence in Summer Meals Campaign, 61

faith-based communities, 143
Family Health Center (McLennan County, TX), 65
family structure, and hunger, 47–48
fear, 102
Federal Emergency Management Agency (FEMA), 1, 3, 5
feeding of the five thousand, 53–55, 140
Fernandez, Maria, 99
food banks, 11
food deserts, 56–57
food insecurity, 44, 45, 57, 71, 77, 113, 127, 132, 142, 145, 150n17
Food Policy Roundtable, 121
Food Stamps Program, 62
food surplus in America, 127
Francis of Assisi, xi, 29, 37, 55, 56, 104

Galvan, Lourdes, 104
Gandhi, Mahatma, 8
global economy, 46
Great Recession (2009), 122
Griggs, Jackson, 65
Guadalupe Street Coffee (San Antonio), 85–89, 95–97, 99, 102, 104
gun violence, 110

Homeland Security, 5
homeless, 30, 63, 70, 141
  and mental health, 148n6
  and substance abuse, 148n7
hope, 142–43
Hope House (Waco), 31–37, 39
hospitality house, 93–94, 98
human dignity, 131
hunger
  as acceptable socioeconomic condition, 141
  and aging, 48–49
  blue and red states on, 123
  complexity of, 116
  as debilitating, 8
  and education, 46–47

as episodic, 45
and family structure, 47–48
and mental health, 48–49
as pressing issue, 21
and race, 48
realities of, 10
systemic response to, 134–35
and underemployment, 45–46
in the United States, 44–50
Hunger Free Community Coalitions, 76, 82–83, 118, 121, 127, 128
hunger ministries, 116
Hurricane Gustav, 5, 6, 7
Hurricane Ike, 5, 6, 7
Hurricane Katrina, 1–5, 7, 10, 143

image of God, 23, 30, 109, 115, 124, 135, 139, 141
immigrants, 114
implementation action plans, 80–82
incarnational organizing, 128
income disparity, 18–19
Indy Hunger Network, 80

Jesus Christ
command to feed the hungry, 66
life of, 27
Johnson, Lyndon, 62
justice, 69, 92–94

Kelly Ingram Park (Birmingham), 29, 143–44
Kennedy, John F., 62
kingdom of God, 41–44, 143
King, Martin Luther, Jr., 23, 83, 100, 117, 139, 140
Klansmen, 144–45
Klein, Ezra, 112
Krey, Kathy, 58, 129

La Fe Community Center (El Paso), 41, 42
Landers, Lacy, 103

Landry, Loretta, 61
"least of these," 141
liberation theology, 38
listening, 90, 95
living on the margins, 25–26
location (action plan), 82
logistical support, 81
Lolita (donkey), 133–34
love
drives out hate, 117
stronger than fear, 102
loving our neighbor, 7, 109
Ludwig, Bill, 118–21, 122, 125, 126, 134
lynching, 139

Maslow's hierarchy of needs, 58, 151n3
Meals on Wheels, 49
Medicaid, 105
mental health, 30, 48–49, 148n6
mission centers, 96
Mission Waco, 56–57
modern complex systems, 72–74

National Commission on Hunger, 40, 46, 110–15
National School Lunch Program, 58
No Kid Hungry Campaign, 61
Nolen, Erin, 58
nonprofits, working together, 70–72

Obama, Barak, 104–5, 112
one-on-one outreach, 77

P3 (public-private partnership), 106–7
Parks, Rosa, 83
Parsons, Talcott, 72, 74, 138
Paul, on interdependence of the body, 73–74
Paynter, Suzii, 119–20, 121
plan for action, 79–80, 121–23
political activism, 103–5

poor
  as clients, 100
  systemic oppression of, 141–42
populism, 19, 20
poverty
  as acceptable socioeconomic condition, 141
  complexity of, 18, 22, 30, 116
  and economic decisions, 141
  as form of violence, 8
  systemic response to, 134–35
poverty issues, 37
power, models of, 67–69
Preble Street organization (Maine), 46
prosperity theology, 51
prostitution, 32, 148n9
Ptacek, Thomas, 63, 64
public and private sectors, 106–7, 123
public shaming, 68–70, 107–8, 116

race, and hunger, 48
racism, 139–50
Radle, Patti, 97
Rauschenbusch, Walter, 148n5
  (chap. 3)
Reconstruction, 20–21
recruiting participants, 76–78, 81,
  118–21
relationships, 77
resources, 81–82
Roosevelt, Franklin Delano, 18

Samford University, 26
San Antonio. See West Side of San
  Antonio
Sanford Social Innovation Review, 14
scapegoating, 50–52, 66, 145
School Breakfast Program (Texas),
  58
school breakfasts, 57–60
segregation, 139
sexual violence, 113–14
shaming power. See public shaming
shared power, 69–70, 75, 106–8

Share Our Strength, 61, 128
Sharkey, Joe, 42–44, 113
slavery, 138, 141
slave trade, 138
snowball effect, 78
social activation, 15
social safety net existence, 20
Southern Baptists, 139
Southland Baptist Church (San Angelo, TX), 12
South Plains Hunger Solutions, 78
Southwest Voter Registration and
  Education Project, 97
Springhill Paper, 19–20
Students for Nonviolent Coordinating Committee, 128
substance abuse, 148n7
summer meals programs, 60–62, 131
Supplemental Nutrition Assistance
  Program (SNAP), 62–64, 105

taking action, 80–82, 127–30
Tanner, Jeff, 129
target dates, 81
tension maintenance, 138
Texas Hunger Initiative (THI), xi, 7,
  11, 12, 57, 58, 70, 76, 79, 105, 115,
  118, 134
Thrifty Food Plan, 63
Together at the Table (Baylor University), 123–24
Tom Green County (Texas), 13–14
tracking (action plan), 82
trade-offs, 49–50
training, 81
Travis Baptist Church (Corpus
  Christi, Texas), 36
Trevino, Dan, 7–8, 61
trickle-up economics, 64
Truett Seminary (Baylor University),
  31, 38
Trump, Donald, 18
trust, collaboration, and commitment, 14, 100, 112, 117, 143

Truth and Reconciliation Commission (South Africa), 48

underemployment, and hunger, 45–46
United States Department of Agriculture (USDA), 11, 119–20, 122

Veggie Prescription Program, 65
Velasquez, Katarina, 96–97
Velasquez, Willie, 96
Villaigosa, Antonio, 104
volunteers, 76, 81

War on Poverty, 62
welfare queen, myth of, 51
West Side of San Antonio, 16, 90–95, 96, 104
Wilberforce, William, 138–39, 140, 145
winner-takes-all battle, 109–10, 112, 117
World Hunger Relief, 64–65

Yellen, Donna, 46